WHO IS THIS KING OF GLORY?

WHO IS THIS KING OF GLORY?

A NEW COMMENTARY
ON THE BOOK OF THE REVELATION

J. J. COMO

BOLD VISION BOOKS
PO BOX 2011
FRIENDSWOOD, TEXAS 77549

ISBN: 9780615891347

Bold Vision Books
PO Box 2011
Friendswood, Texas 77549

Original artwork by Leonard Valeen.
Cover Photo by Leslie Kae Rice.

Published in the United States of America.

DEDICATION

To the One and only true God—the Father, His Son Jesus, and His precious Holy Spirit—be all praise and adoration forevermore.

To my family, each in his or her own manner, who have continually encouraged me in this project. Thank you. A special thanks to my granddaughter for contributing her artistic version of the beast. May God bless each of you for your support.

To my friends who have prayed this endeavor through to completion. Thank you.

To Lyn Valeen for the untold hours spent on the graphics used within these pages.

To my editors who have patiently steered my inadequacies to the full potential of the result of this commentary. Thank you.

TABLE OF CONTENTS

DIAGRAMS

PREFACE

If you are interested in end time study, you know there are numerous books, charts, pamphlets, and movies on the subject. Each one gives views and scenarios and postulates what possibly could happen in the end of days.

So then, why write another book on this seemingly diverse and endless subject? I believe a fresh look at the *Book of the Revelation* is needed. So much has been written and stated, and it seems so complicated. Many are willing to take any opinion of these matters. I challenge you to wipe the slate clean of preconceptions and search with me to discover what the Book of the Revelation actually says.

I encourage you to meditate and ponder with me. Let's ask God to show us the truths as we take the journey through these words. Let's ask Him to help us see what isn't true. Let's enjoy contemplating and understanding the Living Word of the King of Glory.

—J. J. Como

KARA'S
REVELATION 13
BEAST

INTRODUCTION

Oh, how I love a good mystery. When there is a conundrum or dilemma, count me in to try to solve the puzzle and crack the case. I'll follow every clue and trail. The last book of the Bible, The Revelation of Jesus Christ, is a marvelous mystery, which unveils the glory of our Lord Jesus Christ. Join me as we fit all the puzzle pieces and clues together. When we are done, we will display an accurate and proper picture of the One who is coming to rule and reign. He will have the keys of authority over death and Hades. He is the King of kings, the Lord of lords, and the King of Glory.

Our template for the investigation will be the twenty-seventh book of the New Testament because this manuscript by the Apostle John gives us the most information concerning Jesus Christ's unveiling. Through John's writings, we will investigate His marvelous mystery.

Glossary

APOSTASY   A total desertion of or departure from principles, party, cause, etc.

BEAST   A symbolic animal used to illustrate kingdoms of the world

BEAST KINGDOM
A symbolic creature that has characteristics of animal parts used to illustrate kingdoms of the world

ESCHATOLOGY
The doctrines of last or final things, such as death, the judgment, the future state, etc

FALSE PROPHET
One who dishonestly assumes the work of a prophet, teaching false doctrines in the name of God

FATHER GOD
The One Supreme Being, the creator and ruler of the universe

GLORIFIED BODY
A heavenly spiritual form or body, incorruptible, imperishable, and immortal, which a believer in Jesus receives at resurrection

HOLY SPIRIT   The Spirit of the Living God

INDUCTIVE   Pertaining to or employing logical explanations for a set of particular facts; a conclusion reached by this process

JESUS   Son of God, born of a virgin, God in the flesh; the Savior of mankind

JIHAD   A war with a religious object by Islamists upon others; a violent crusade against any belief other than Islam

MYSTERY   Anything kept secret or remaining unexplained or unknown

PARCHMENT PAPER
The skin of sheep or goats prepared for use as a writing material for manuscripts or documents

THE APPEARANCE

The Roman emperor Domitian exiled the beloved Apostle John to the Isle of Patmos after John had served Jesus as one of His twelve most trusted followers. In John's isolation, Jesus appeared as the One standing amid seven golden lampstands.

Do not be afraid; I am the First and the Last.

> Then I turned to see the voice that spoke with me. And having turned I saw seven golden lampstands, and in the midst of the seven lampstands One like the Son of Man, clothed with a garment down to the feet and girded about the chest with a golden band. His head and hair were white like wool, as white as snow, and His eyes like a flame of fire; His feet were like fine brass, as if refined in a furnace, and His voice as the sound of many waters; He had in His right hand seven stars, out of His mouth went a sharp two-edged sword, and His countenance was like the sun shining in its strength. And when I saw Him, I fell at His feet as dead. But He laid His right hand on me, saying to me, "Do not be afraid; I am the First and the Last. I am He who lives, and was dead, and behold, I am alive forevermore. Amen" (Revelation 1:12-18 NKJV).

Jesus appeared as if He was clad in a floor-length robe with a golden sash. He had white hair and a white head; His face shone as the sun; His eyes were flaming and His feet glowing. The appearance of Christ's glory overwhelmed John; he fell as if dead at the feet of the Savior.

How did John recognize Jesus? In the flesh, John knew Him well. John was one of Jesus' closest selected disciples. For three years they walked in Israel and lived together as comrades and Jesus mentored the twelve disciples in the ways of the Kingdom of God. Jesus, as a man, had "no appearance so as to be attracted to Him" (Isaiah 53:2). Yet John stated in his gospel account that he had beheld Jesus' earthly "glory, full of grace and truth." (See John 1:14.)

At the bitter end of Jesus' life, John witnessed, close at hand, all that Jesus suffered physically. There was the crown of thorns pressed into His head, the purple robe which adorned His body, the bloodshed from the lashings and the nails in His hands, and the piercing of His side by a spear. John stood nearby as a witness to all the final events leading to Jesus' death. Then shortly after the resurrection, Jesus came to stand among the disciples. He identified Himself by showing them the scars on His hands and side. John had seen Jesus as a man and in Jesus' glorified body after the resurrection.

Even though the Revelation chapter one text does not mention Jesus' hands and side, the description identifies Jesus as the "Son of Man," the "First and the Last…who lives, and was dead, and…alive forevermore." All these descriptions are identification—proof of who Jesus is.

In addition, there is a recorded account of John seeing Jesus in His glorified body before the cross. This event is similar to the Revelation account. In Matthew 17:2, Jesus was "transfigured before three disciples [John, James, and Peter], and His face shone like the sun, and His garments became as white as light." Because of this manifestation of Jesus before His resurrection and John's eyewitness of Jesus' resurrection, John recognized Jesus in this glorified state on the Isle of Patmos.

Blessed is the one who reads, hears, and heeds.

In this vision, Jesus commissioned John to write to the Bride of Christ about the things John would behold with his own eyes in the Spirit. These future events concern the return of the Lord back to this sin-affected earth. Everyone living at that tumultuous time will witness Jesus' glorious return as ruler over the kings of the earth and will mourn their personal rejection of His gracious salvation.

Many think that the Book of Revelation is far too difficult to understand, but may I encourage you; for if we read and hear with understanding and heed the things written therein, Jesus promises a blessing.

> Blessed is he who reads and those who hear the words of this prophecy, and keep those things which are written in it; for the time is near (Revelation 1:3 NKJV).

If we study and know the Book of Revelation,

1. We will not be tossed to and fro or here and there in doctrine when tumultuous things begin to happen on the earth.

2. We will be enabled to persevere in the Lord until the end whether by death or life or the catching away of the Church to be with the Lord.

3. We will have insight and understanding about the things occurring on earth in order to bring more people into the Kingdom of God, so they will not have to endure the wrath of God.

4. We will be able to answer questions from those who fear the afflictions to come on the earth, because these things must take place to usher in the ruling Kingdom of God.

5. We will warn, with conviction and compassion, unbelievers about the wrath to come.

6. We will know without a doubt that the Lord and Savior, Jesus, is coming back soon in all His majesty and glory.

Look, I am coming soon! My reward is with me, and I will give to each person according to what they have done. Revelation 22:12 NET

Deuteronomy 19:15b admonishes that all is established by the mouth of two or more witnesses. Therefore, Jesus' coming back to the earth is clearly established by the word of God through three witnesses in Scripture. These witnesses include Jesus, angels, and the disciple who penned Hebrews. Jesus reminds readers of His coming in John 14:1-3, Matthew 24:27-30, and Revelation 22:12.

Do not let your hearts be distressed. You believe in God; believe also in me. There are many dwelling places in my Father's house. Otherwise, I would have told you, because I am going away to make ready a place for you. And if I go and make ready a place for you, I will come again and take you to be with me, so that where I am you may be too (John 14:1-3 NET).

For just like the lightning comes from the east and flashes to the west, so the coming of the Son of Man will be. Wherever the corpse is, there the vultures will gather. Immediately after the suffering of those days, the sun will be darkened, and the moon will not give its light; the stars will fall from heaven, and the powers of heaven will be shaken. Then the sign of the Son of Man will appear in heaven, and all the tribes of the earth will mourn. They will see the Son of Man arriving on the clouds of heaven with power and great glory (Matthew 24:27-30 NET).

In addition, angels verified the truth of His coming in Acts 1:9-11.

After he had said this, while they were watching, he was lifted up and a cloud hid him from their sight. As they were still staring into the sky while he was going, suddenly two men (angels) in white clothing stood near them and said, "Men of Galilee, why do you stand here looking up into the sky? This same Jesus who has been taken up from you into heaven will come back in the same way you saw him go into heaven" (NET).

Also, Hebrews 9:27-28 enforces the truth of His coming.

> And just as people are appointed to die once, and then to face judgment, so also, after Christ was offered once to bear the sins of many, to those who eagerly await him he will appear a second time, not to bear sin but to bring salvation (NET).

We must be ready for the imminent coming of the Lord Jesus Christ. Father God is clear in the first verse of the Revelation. He wants His bondservants to see and know what must shortly take place.

> The Revelation of Jesus Christ, which God gave Him to show His servants—things which must shortly take place. And He sent and signified it by His angel to His servant John (Revelation 1:1 NKJV).

The text calls us servants. A better rendering of the word "servants" is bondservants. Historically, a bondservant was no ordinary servant or slave. A bondservant was a slave or servant who had been freed, but because of the love he had for his master, chose to continue in servitude. With this understanding, the rendering of bondservant here relates to a believer's love and devotion to Jesus Christ. Because Jesus released us from the slavery to sin, we choose to continue to serve the Master Jesus out of love.

What God desires His bondservants to be shown, I desire to see. So, together let's look at the clues, signs, evidences, and puzzle pieces so we may see a clear and correct picture as portrayed in the Revelation of Jesus the Christ.

This commentary is unlike others you may have read. To know God and His Word in a deep way, we must do more than merely read Scripture and study what someone else has to say about it. I believe too many of us read the commentaries instead of the Word. It is my hope to see what the Scripture actually says about these end times. I have tried to approach the events in the Book of Revelation without preconceived ideas.

I did not start with a notion or theory about eschatology—the study of end times. I have not predetermined or defined any time periods, places, or ideas. Instead, together we will read and accept the words as they are written. We will make lists of what the verses actually say instead of what we think they mean. We will let the Scripture guide us to a conclusion. The method used to achieve the conclusions is derived from an inductive way of studying the Word of God. The meaning of inductive is to "reason from particular facts to come to a general conclusion." Along with the inspired Bible, our Teacher, the Holy Spirit, leads us into all truth and reveals the things of God to us. Then understanding is achieved. The Bible becomes its own commentary. After fully observing what the Scripture says, we'll then search out other Scriptures in order to find out what the whole counsel of the Word of God reveals. Scripture never contradicts Scripture.

I will show you what must take place.

Revelation 1:19 divides John's manuscript into three parts:

1. The things which John has seen (Chapter 1).
2. The things which are (Chapters 2-3).
3. The things which shall take place after these things (Chapters 4-22).

> Write the things which thou hast seen, and the things which are, and the things which shall be hereafter (Revelation 1:19 KJV).

For our investigation we will focus on the last section—the "things which shall take place after these things." These are the future events (beginning in Revelation chapter 4) that are to take place in and on the earth soon.

> After these things, I looked and behold, a door standing open in heaven, and the first voice which I had heard, like the sound of a trumpet speaking with me said, "Come up here, and I will show you what must take place after these things" (Revelation 4:1 NASB).

2 THE BREAKING OF THE SEALS (THE ONE)

The fourth chapter of the Book of the Revelation introduces us to the One sitting on a throne in heaven.

> Immediately I was in the Spirit; and behold, a throne set in heaven, and One sat on the throne. And He who sat there was like a jasper and a sardius stone in appearance; and there was a rainbow around the throne, in appearance like an emerald. Around the throne were twenty-four thrones, and on the thrones I saw twenty-four elders sitting, clothed in white robes; and they had crowns of gold on their heads. And from the throne proceeded lightnings, thunderings, and voices. Seven lamps of fire were burning before the throne, which are the seven Spirits of God (Revelation 4:2–5 NKJV).

Holy, Holy, Holy is the Lord God...He holds a scroll with seven seals.

The One sitting on the throne is different than the One described in Revelation chapter one. Notice the distinctions between them. The One here in the chapter 4 text is called the Lord God. Surrounding the throne are twenty-four elders and four living creatures. According to verses 6-8, they continuously worship the One on the throne, and never cease saying, "Holy, Holy, Holy is the Lord God." Credit is given to Him as Creator of all (in verse 11). In His right hand, He holds a scroll with seven seals.

> And I saw in the right hand of Him who sat on the throne a scroll written inside and on the back, sealed with seven seals (Revelation 5:1 NKJV).

In the ancient world, written communication was on parchment paper, often on the front and the back of each page. The parchment documents would then be rolled up. A seal would be placed on the visible edge to assure privacy or security and to guarantee the scrolls' genuineness. In all of heaven, there is only one person found worthy to open the scroll with the seven seals. That person is Jesus.

This scroll is perhaps the title deed to the earth, gained back from the devil at Jesus' resurrection, giving Him all authority over heaven and earth.

> Jesus came up and spoke to them saying, "All authority has been given to Me in heaven and on earth" (Matthew 28:18 NASB).

The only One worthy is the Lamb of God who was slain and "has overcome, so as to open the scroll and its seals."[1] (See Revelation 5:5.)

> And they sang a new song, saying: "You are worthy to take the scroll and to open its seals, because you were slain, and with your blood you purchased for God persons from every tribe and language and people and nation (Revelation 5:9 NIV).

The Lamb, Jesus the Christ, is the Kinsman Redeemer,[2] who liberated believers from slavery and bondage to sin, who redeemed believers from the loss of the land, the whole earth, and who avenged believers from the murderer who brought about man's death on the earth—Satan. With His blood, the Lamb redeemed, or purchased, individuals from every race of peoples. Because He overcame as the Kinsman Redeemer of mankind, the Lamb is worthy to receive "power, riches, wisdom, honor, might, glory, and blessing" (Revelation 5:12 NASB) and He alone is eligible to open the seals.

In Revelation chapter 6, the worthy Lamb opens six of the seven seals in consecutive order, one at a time. Each seal initiates a command from the Lamb in heaven resulting in an event happening on earth.

❶ Seal One

A rider on a white horse holds a bow and wears a crown; he goes out conquering and to conquer. (See Revelation 6:1-2.) The bow symbolizes a weapon of war and the crown is given for military valor. Evidence perhaps points to this rider being the Islamic religion movement, especially the attempt to make Muslim converts in almost all parts of the world—including in prisons, by Muslims marrying Christian women, by natural offspring increasing Muslim populations, and by the rise of Jihad, the militant forcing of a country or part of a country to obey the laws of Islam.

❷ Seal Two

A red horse rider with a sword takes peace from the earth so that men slay one another. (See Revelation 6:3-4.) When we examine the violence of radical Islam, it seems to fit the idea of peace being removed from the earth as seen in the "Arab Spring" movements in the Middle East where rioting was commonplace. Nothing in history has taken peace from the world like the threat of Islamic Jihad terrorist activity.

❸ Seal Three

A black horse rider has a pair of scales that causes an imbalance and price inflation of basic foodstuffs such as grain. (See Revelation 6:5-6.) Global economic upheaval will be rampant in all nations. Current financial markets in many countries, including the United States, exhibit economic upheaval. Reports of bail-outs for entire governments flood the news. Strange weather patterns have caused worldwide shortages in crops of corn, wheat, and other foods to drive prices up. Because of close intertwining in economics of the whole world, one country's lack of output of grains and commodities affects many countries negatively. Exports and imports of these goods can come to a halt.

❹ Seal Four

A rider on an ashen horse is named death, with hades following. He kills one-fourth of the earth with sword, famine, pestilence, and wild beasts (See Revelation 6:7-8.) This seal likely pertains to unbelievers because Death and Hades have no power over believers. A possible means to achieve these outcomes could be war.

These four horsemen appear to be spiritual entities but have an authority or ability for a physical manifestation on earth. The reasoning for this conclusion concerning the spiritual entities stems from a passage in Zechariah 6:5, 7 listing the same horse colors as these in Revelation 6. When Zechariah asked who these were he was told, "These are four spirits of heaven" and "strong ones… who patrol the earth." Thus, I think the riders are spiritual beings sent out to complete a task. The Lamb commands the horsemen to come forth to achieve their purpose on the earth. The Lamb is exerting His authority concerning these riders. The Lamb has full control of the events, giving limited authority to the horsemen, such as economic upheaval and men killing and being killed.

❺ Seal Five

Under the altar, souls, slain for the Word of God who maintained their testimony, are given a white robe in heaven and told to wait for the rest of the martyrs who are to be killed. (See Revelation 6:9-11) The victims appear to be Jewish martyrs since there is no mention of Jesus and the fact that the Jewish people were entrusted with the oracles of God to maintain the writings of the Word of God. (See Romans 3:2.) Jews maintain and preserve the writings of the old covenants while looking forward to the appearing of the Messiah.

❻ Seal Six

A great worldwide earthquake causes the sun to appear black and the moon to appear red; the stars fall to the earth; the sky splits apart like a scroll. (See Revelation 6:12-17.) These huge disasters are a fulfillment of Isaiah's prophecy.

> All the host of heaven will wear away, the sky will be rolled up like a scroll; all their hosts will also wither away as a leaf withers from the vine or as one withers from the fig tree (Isaiah 34:4 NASB).

Then every mountain and island move and men hide in caves. These events are a fulfillment of another of Isaiah's prophecies.

> "Men will go into caves of the rocks and into holes of the ground before the splendor of His majesty, when He arises to make the earth tremble. In that day men will cast away to moles and bats their idols of silver and gold, which they made for themselves to worship in order to go into the caverns of the rocks and the clefts of the cliffs, before the terror of the LORD and the splendor of His majesty, when He arises to make the earth tremble (Isaiah 2:19-21 NASB).

The events surrounding seal six are so severe that the people think the "wrath of God" (Revelation 6:17) has come.

While seals one through three are somewhat generic, we can attribute the events listed above as possibilities that these seals have already been opened. However, because of their specific harshness, we can be certain that seals four through six have not occurred.

After the sixth seal of the scroll is opened, a halt takes place. An angel intervenes to stop the opening of the seventh seal.[3] The angel carries the seal, or mark of the Living God, and with it seals or marks the foreheads of the bondservants of God. These sealed ones total 144,000—12,000 males from each tribe of Israel (Judah, Reuben, Gad, Asher, Naphtali, Manasseh, Simeon, Levi, Issachar, Zebulum, Ephraim, and Benjamin). (See Revelation 7:1-8.)

3   THE GREAT MULTITUDE REVEALED

Revelation 7 reflects the fulfillment of the new covenant in heaven.

> After these things I looked, and behold, a great multitude which no one could count, from every nation and all tribes and peoples and tongues, standing before the throne and before the Lamb, clothed in white robes, and palm branches were in their hands; and they cry out with a loud voice, saying, "Salvation to our God who sits on the throne, and to the Lamb." And all the angels were standing around the throne and around the elders and the four living creatures; and they fell on their faces before the throne and worshiped God, saying, "Amen, blessing and glory and wisdom and thanksgiving and honor and power and might, be to our God forever and ever. Amen." Then one of the elders answered, saying to me, "These who are clothed in the white robes, who are they, and where have they come from?" I said to him, "My Lord, you know." And he said to me, "These are the ones who come out of the great tribulation, and they have washed their robes and made them white in the blood of the Lamb. For this reason, they are before the throne of God; and they serve him day and night in His temple; and He who sits on the throne will spread His tabernacle over them. They will hunger no longer, nor thirst anymore; nor will the sun beat down on them, nor any heat; for the Lamb in the center of the throne will be their shepherd, and will guide them to the springs of the water of life; and God will wipe away every tear from their eyes" (Revelation 7:9-17 NASB).

Revelation seven reflects the fulfillment of the New Covenant in heaven.

After the sealing of the 144,000 Israelites, a great multitude from every nation, tribe, people, and language stands before God's throne and the Lamb in heaven. This great multitude is clothed in white robes, having "washed their robes and made them white in the blood of the Lamb."[4] Also, in their hands are palm branches, which might indicate the celebration of the Feast of Tabernacles as

Father God spreads His tabernacle over them. The Lamb of God will be their Shepherd.

Numerous reasons convince us that this great multitude seen in heaven at this time is the church, the Bride of Christ. This multitude of peoples has been caught up to be with God in His tabernacle and with the Bridegroom, Jesus Christ. These facts about the church point to this conclusion.

The church, the Bride of Christ, includes every nation, tribe, people, and tongue.

◆ The church, the Bride of Christ, includes every nation, tribe, people, and tongue. (See Revelation 5:9.)

◆ The church, the Bride of Christ, has been washed in the blood of the Lamb of God, the Lord Jesus. (See Revelation 19:8-14; 22:14.)

◆ The church has been saved through Father God and Jesus' plan. (See Acts 4:12; Romans 4:16; Revelation 1:5-6; 1 Thessalonians 5:9.)

◆ Jesus promised the overcomers of the church that they would never go out of the temple (tabernacle) of God. (See Revelation 3:12.)

◆ The depiction of God spreading His tabernacle over them is a fulfillment of covenant promises of covering illustrated in the Feast of Tabernacles. (See Leviticus 23:40; Deuteronomy 16:13-15.)

◆ The listing of the food and drink is a reference to the fulfillment of the new covenant with the Lord Jesus by partaking of the bread and the wine. (See John 6:35.)

◆ The church is the first to experience Father God wiping away every tear from their eyes. (See Isaiah 25:7-9; 49:10; Revelation 21:4.)

The Bride of Christ is caught away so that believers may dwell with the Lord Jesus and with Father God. According to Revelation 19:6-7, the Bride of Christ is identified as the great multitude, the bondservants of God.

Diagram: THE GREAT MULTITUDE IS THE CHURCH - PAGE 27

THE GREAT MULTITUDE IS THE CHURCH

From Revelation 7	From other Biblical Prophecies
7:9 – "...from every nation, all tribes, peoples, tongues."	**Revelation 5:9** – "... for You (Jesus) were slain and did purchase for God with Your blood from every tribe, tongue, people and nation."
7:9, 14 – "...clothed in white robes, washed and made white in the blood of the Lamb."	**Revelation 19:8, 14** – "It was given to her (the Bride) to clothe herself in fine linen, bright and clean; for the fine linen is the righteous acts of the saints. The armies ... in heaven, clothed in fine linen, white and clean, were following Him (Jesus) ..."
	Revelation 22:14 – "Blessed are those who wash their robes ..."
7:10 – "Salvation belongs (is due) to our God and the Lamb."	**Acts 4:12** – "There is salvation in no one else; ... no other name ... by which we must be saved."
	Romans 1:16 – "... the gospel for it is the power of God for salvation to everyone who believes."
	Revelation 1:5, 6 – "... Jesus Christ ... who loves us and released us from our sins by His blood, and has made us to be a kingdom, priests to his God and Father."
	1 Thessalonians 5:9 – "... God has destined us for ... obtaining salvation."
7:15 – "Serve God day and night in His temple."	**Revelation 3:12** – "He who overcomes I will make him a pillar in the temple of God and he will not go out from it anymore." (a promise to the churches)
7:16 – "...shall hunger no more or thirst anymore ..." (shows partaking of the elements of covenant, bread and drink, and the fulfillment of that covenant)	**Psalm 107:9** – The LORD "has satisfied the thirsty soul, and the hungry soul He has filled with what is good."
	Isaiah 49:10 – "They will not hunger or thirst, neither will the scorching heat or sun strike them down..."
	John 6:35 – "Jesus said, 'I am the bread of life; he who comes to Me shall not hunger and he who believes in Me shall never thirst.'"
7:17 – "...shall guide them to springs of the water of life and God shall wipe every tear from their eyes."	**Isaiah 25:7-9** – "...He will swallow up death for all time, and the LORD God will wipe tears away from all faces..."
	Isaiah 49:10 – The LORD "... will lead them and will guide them to springs of water."
	Revelation 21:4 – "He shall wipe away every tear from their eyes..."
The scriptures in **Revelation 7:9-17** reflect the fulfillment of the New Covenant to believers in heaven by the catching away of the Bride of Christ, so that we may forever be with the Lord, and the Father to dwell among us!	

The initial reward for the overcoming Church, the Bride of Christ, is the promise of the catching away to meet the Bridegroom. Three passages in the New Testament describe the catching away of the Bride of Christ, the Church.

First, Jesus reminds the disciples that He is going away "to prepare a place" and "will come again to receive you to myself, that where I am you may be also." (See John 14:1-3.) Then the Apostle Paul states that not all believers will experience death, but that some believers will "be changed in a moment" to be "imperishable" along with those already dead (asleep) in Christ. (See 1 Corinthians 15:51-54.) Paul also affirms that the "dead in Christ will rise first" then those "alive will be caught up with them" to "meet the Lord in the air" in the clouds. (See 1 Thessalonians 4:13-18.)

The Lord has promised the church that He will "deliver us (believers) from the wrath to come" (1 Thessalonians 1:10) and be "kept from the hour (time) of testing which is about to come upon the whole world" (Revelation 3:10) because "God has not destined us for wrath" (1 Thessalonians 5:9). The timing of the catching away of the Bride of Christ coincides with the great multitude appearing in heaven and worshiping before the Throne of God in Revelation 7:9-17. The diagram *The Rapture of the Church* lists other timing clues about the catching away of the Church.[5]

Diagram: THE RAPTURE OF THE CHURCH - PAGE 29

The ultimate timing of the rapture is prophesied more precisely in the Levitical feasts of Israel called Passover, Unleavened Bread, Firstfruits, Pentecost, Trumpets, Atonement, and Tabernacles. The first four feasts—which include Passover, Unleavened Bread, Firstfruits, and Pentecost—were fulfilled by Jesus through his first coming when he came to live and die on earth.

Concerning Passover, Jesus became the sacrificial lamb by shedding His blood and applying the blood to the door posts of the heart so that death would pass over. On the day of Unleavened Bread, Jesus as the Bread of Life removed the leaven of sin by shedding His blood on the cross. And on the day of Firstfruits, Jesus was first to be raised from the dead overcoming death with the promise of a harvest of souls, so that many more would be raised from the dead. Then, on Pentecost, the Holy Spirit was given to believers. Jesus will fulfill the last three feasts—Feasts of Trumpets, Atonement, and Tabernacles—with equal precision in His second coming.
The first of the coming feasts is called Trumpets which coincides with the

The Rapture of the Church

"Catching Away" References	"Catching Away" Timing Clues
In My Father's house are many dwellings, I go to prepare a place for you; I will come again & receive you to Myself, that where I am you may be also (John 14:1-3)	Jesus will deliver us from the wrath to come (1 Thess. 1:10)
	God did not destine the church for wrath (1 Thess. 5:9)
We shall not all sleep, we shall all be changed. In a moment... the trumpet shall sound, dead will be raised imperishable & we will be changed... death is swallowed up in victory (1 Cor. 15:51-54)	Church kept from the hour of testing which comes upon the unbelievers (Rev. 3:10)
	Day of the Lord (not the Rapture) will not come unless the Restrainer (Dan. 12:1) is taken out of the way (2 Thess. 2:6-7)
	John saw bad things which take place after the Churches (Rev. chapters 8-18)
Lord will descend from heaven with a shout with the trumpet of God, & the dead in Christ shall rise first. Then those alive & remaining shall be caught up together with them in the clouds to meet the Lord in the air... (1 Thess. 4:16-18)	Those with Jesus (at His Coming) are the called, chosen, & faithful (Rev. 17:14)
	The Bride is dressed in fine linen (Rev. 19:8)
	Jesus' army clothed in fine linen (Rev. 19:14)

blowing of the trumpets to call the Bride home to heaven in the rapture. For a better description of all the feasts and how Jesus has fulfilled or is going to fulfill each one, see the following:

Diagrams: God's Feasts of Israel (1 & 2) - Pages 31-32

The Church, the Bride of Christ, includes all those who overcome in this life through faith in the redemptive work of Jesus' death, burial, and triumphant resurrection. Jesus promises to give many rewards to the overcoming Church including:

1. Jesus will grant an overcomer to eat of the tree of life located in the paradise of God. (See Revelation 2:7.)

2. An overcomer will not be hurt by the second death, which is the partaking of the lake of fire, but will receive the crown of life. (See Revelation 2:10-11.)

3. Jesus will give an overcomer some of the hidden manna and be given a white stone with a new unknown name written on it. (See Revelation 2:17.)

4. An overcomer will be given authority to rule. (See Revelation 2:26-28.)

5. An overcomer will be clothed in white garments symbolizing righteousness and Jesus will confess his name before His Father and His angels. (See Revelation 3:5.)

6. Jesus will make an overcomer a pillar in God's temple and will write on him God's name, Jesus' new name, and the name of the city New Jerusalem. (See Revelation 3:12.)

These rewards are wonderful and grand privileges.

God's Feasts of Israel (1)

	Festival of Pesach, 1st Month (Nisan)				Festival of Shavuot, 3rd Month (Sivan)
	Passover	Unleavened Bread	Firstfruits		Pentecost, Feast of Weeks
Israel was a slave in Egypt	Kill the lamb, and put blood on your doorposts. (Ex. 12:6-7) 1st month, 14th day (Lev. 23:5)	Purge out the old leaven (sin symbol) from your houses (Ex. 12:15-20) 1st month, 15th day for 7 days: sabbath (Lev. 23:6-9)	Wave offering of the 1st sheave (harvest promise) (Ex. 23:16-19) 1st month, 23rd day (Lev. 23:10-14)	Plants grow in Israel	Wave Offering by priest of 2 loaves of leavened bread (fruit of the harvest) (Ex. 34:22 & Deut. 16:10) 50 days (7 weeks + 1 day) after firstfruits (Lev. 23:15-21)
Whoever commits sin is a slave to sin. (Jn. 8.34)	Christ our passover has been sacrificed. (1 Cor. 5:7)	Clean out the old leaven... let us celebrate the feast (1 Cor. 5:7-8)	Christ has been raised from the dead the firstfruits... (1 Cor. 15 :21-23)	Going away so that Comforter can come. (Jn. 16:17)	Coming of the Holy Spirit on this day The mystery of the church - Jew & Gentile in one body (Acts 2:1-43, Eph. 3:4-9)

God's Feasts of Israel (2)

Festival of Succoth , during the Seventh Month (Tishri)		
Feast of Trumpets	Day of Atonement	Feast of Tabernacles
Trumpets blown A holy convocation Offer a burnt offering (Num. 29:1-6) 7th month, first day (Lev. 23:23-25)	Atonement shall be made to cleanse you of all sin as a sabbath of solemn rest (Lev. 16:29-31) 7th month, 10th day (Lev. 23:26-32)	Harvest celebration memorial of booths in the wilderness (Lev. 16:13-16) 7th month, 15th day (Lev. 23:33-44)
Jesus gathering His bride (the church) to Himself as a result of the rapture (1 Cor. 15:51-52) (1 Thess. 4:16-17)	Israel will repent & accept Jesus as Messiah & faithfully follow Him (Zec. 14:3-11) (Rom. 11:25-29)	Families will come to Jerusalem to celebrate this feast with Jesus as King (Zec. 14:16-19)

The Opening of the Seventh Seal

❼ Seal Seven

There is silence in heaven for one half hour.

Following the catching away of the great multitude to heaven, Jesus breaks the seventh seal. The scroll now can be fully opened to reveal the writings (prophecies) in the scroll, written on both the front and back.

DIAGRAM: THE SEVEN SEALS - PAGE 34

The opening of the seventh seal starts the paused timer and begins the last seven years on earth until Jesus Christ returns to claim the earth and to avenge the shed blood of the saints.

This seven years is the last of seventy weeks of years prophesied in Daniel.

> Seventy weeks have been determined concerning your people and your holy city to put an end to rebellion, to bring sin to completion, to atone for iniquity, to bring in perpetual righteousness, to seal up the prophetic vision, and to anoint a most holy place. So know and understand: From the issuing of the command to restore and rebuild Jerusalem until an anointed one, a prince arrives, there will be a period of seven weeks and sixty-two weeks. It will again be built, with plaza and moat, but in distressful times. Now after the sixty-two weeks, an anointed one will be cut off and have nothing. As for the city and the sanctuary, the people of the coming prince will destroy them. But his end will come speedily like a flood. Until the end of the war that has been decreed there will be destruction. He will confirm a covenant with many for one week. But in the

The Revelation Of Jesus Christ

The Seven Seals

WHITE HORSE:
Rider goes out conquering and to conquer: possibly Satan's evil kingdom of Islam

RED HORSE:
Rider granted to take peace from the earth: possibly war

BLACK HORSE:
Rider had pair of scales in hand: possibly famine

ASHEN HORSE:
Rider Death & Hades following granted to kill 1/4 of the earth with sword, famine, sickness, and wild beasts

SOULS UNDER ALTAR:
Souls killed for testimony of God in Heaven

GREAT EARTHQUAKE:
Sun become black and moon red, stars of the sky fall to the earth, 144,000 Jews sealed, Great multitude in heaven

SILENCE IN HEAVEN:
After half hour, angel takes censer with incense & prayers of saints and throws it to the earth; seven angels prepare to sound seven trumpets

All seven seals will have been broken by the Lamb to expose the prophesies written on the inside and back side of the scroll. These prophecies cannot occur until all the seals are broken to open the scroll. (Matt. 24:33, Mark 13:29, Luke 21:31)

middle of that week he will bring sacrifices and offerings to a halt. On the wing of abominations will come one who destroys, until the decreed end is poured out on the one who destroys (Daniel 9:24-27 NET).

God decreed Daniel's people, the Jewish race, and the Holy City (Jerusalem) seventy sevens of years. These 490 years were allotted to

1. finish the transgression,
2. make an end to sin,
3. make atonement for iniquity,
4. bring in everlasting righteousness,
5. seal up vision and prophecy, and
6. anoint the most Holy Place.

With the captivity of the Jews by Babylon in Daniel's time, the promise of the Jewish people to return to their land of Israel became a reality in 454 BC with the decree of King Cyrus of Persia to rebuild Jerusalem. The time clock started in order for the six requirements (above) to be fulfilled. The Jews lived in the land and rebuilt Jerusalem. After 483 years passed, Jesus was born and announced as the Jews' Messiah, but He was rejected as their King, so God paused the countdown clock leaving seven more years to fulfill all the requirements promised to Daniel. God then set up a gap of time to establish the church. When the seventh seal is broken by the Lamb Jesus, the time clock restarts and the last remaining seven years will continue to finish out the Jewish decree.

Jesus was rejected as King of the Jews, so God paused the countdown clock.

These six requirements concerning the Jewish people and their Holy City have not been fully realized as of yet. In order for all of the above requirements to be fulfilled, seven more years must be finished. Only sixty-nine sevens of years (483 years) have been fulfilled as Jesus Christ did not come into His kingdom because of the rejection of the Jewish nation. Therefore, we are now in a gap of time (considered the Church Age consisting of Jew and Non-Jew) until the seventieth seven of years (the last seven years) begins to occur. When these final seven years begin, the fully opened scroll brings about an entire fulfillment of the prophecies in Daniel's seventieth seven of years.

Daniel predicts a prince will make a seven-year covenant with the Jewish people, but then he will break this agreement in the middle of the seven years. We will examine this prince closer when we see the beast in Revelation 13.

Diagram: DANIEL'S 70 SEVENS - PAGE 36

Daniel's 70 Sevens
(of years = 490 years) (9:24-27)

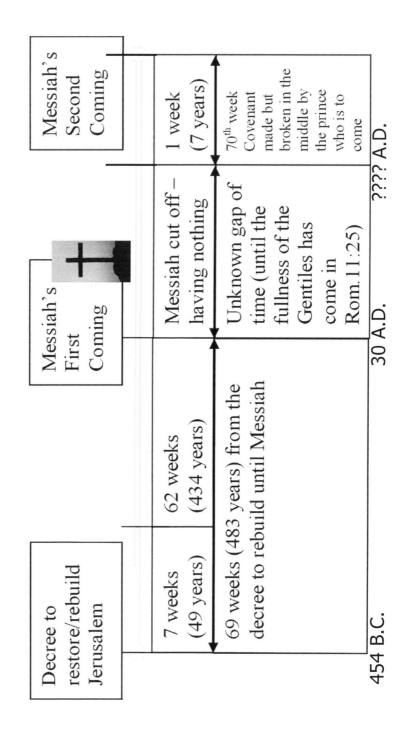

Decree to restore/rebuild Jerusalem		Messiah's First Coming	Messiah's Second Coming
7 weeks (49 years)	62 weeks (434 years)	Messiah cut off – having nothing	1 week (7 years)
69 weeks (483 years) from the decree to rebuild until Messiah		Unknown gap of time (until the fullness of the Gentiles has come in Rom. 11:25)	70th week Covenant made but broken in the middle by the prince who is to come
454 B.C.		30 A.D.	???? A.D.

5 THE SOUNDING OF TRUMPETS

The Lamb finally breaks all seven seals of the scroll to expose the prophesies written on the inside and back side of the scroll. These prophecies cannot occur until all the seals are broken to open the scroll "even so you too, when you see all these things, recognize that He is near, right at the door" (Luke 21:31). (Also see Matthew 24:33 and Mark 13:29.) Continuing in Revelation chapters 8 and 9, with the breaking of the seventh seal, seven angels appear prepared to sound seven trumpets from heaven.

> ▶ Trumpet One sounds and brings hail and fire (brimstone) to earth. One-third of the earth and trees burn along with all the grass. (See Revelation 8:7.)

> ▶ Trumpet Two sounds and sends a mass of fire into the sea. One-third of the seas become blood and one-third of the sea's creatures die along with the destruction of one-third of ships. (See Revelation 8:8-9.) This mass of fire appears to be an asteroid that falls into the sea.

> ▶ Trumpet Three sounds and a burning great star named Wormwood falls from the sky onto one-third of the rivers and springs of water. The bitter poisoned waters cause many men to die. (See Revelation 8:10-11.)

> ▶ Trumpet Four sounds and darkens one-third of the sun, moon, and stars. (See Revelation 8:12.)

Next, an angel sounds a warning concerning the last three soundings of the fifth, sixth, and seventh trumpets. These final trumpets are woeful to those who then dwell on the earth.

> ▶ Trumpet Five sounds and the abyss opens to expel demonic creatures described as locusts. These locusts are not like any ever seen on earth for these appear as horses with gold crowns and human faces with long hair

Seven angels appear prepared to sound seven trumpets from heaven.

and like a lion. Their tails have stingers as scorpions and the power to hurt and torment men for five months. The locusts have no authority to kill, even though those afflicted long for death. Also, the locusts are not permitted to harm the 144,000 Jews sealed or marked unto God. These demonic creatures have a king over them named Abaddon (in Hebrew) or Apollyon (in Greek). His name means "destroyer." This fifth trumpet is the first woe with two more coming (Revelation 9:1-12).

A strong angel had another scroll in his hand.

▶ Trumpet Six sounds and four evil angels arise from the Euphrates River at the appointed time to kill one third of humankind with an army of two hundred million. This army seems to be a demonic force because of the description of the horses; their heads look like lions with fire, smoke, and brimstone coming from their mouths, and their tails look like serpents. The two thirds not killed by the army refuse to repent of their evil deeds. (See Revelation 9:13-21.) Notice where the demonic angels come from, the Euphrates River, located in Iraq—a bastion of Islam.

> And I saw another strong angel coming down out of heaven, clothed with a cloud; and the rainbow was upon his head, and his face was like the sun, and his feet like pillars of fire; and he had in his hand a little book [scroll] which was open. And he placed his right foot on the sea and his left on the land (Revelation 10:1-2 NASB).

Following the sounding of the six trumpets, a strong angel appears on the scene. (See Revelation 10.) Some believe this angel to be Jesus, but I believe it is Michael, the angel guardian over Israel. The creature described as a strong angel is not Jesus, because Jesus is not an angel. Daniel 12:1 states that Michael is the great prince who stands guard over the people of Israel. A similar depiction of the angel speaking to Daniel shows the angel with raised right and left hand toward heaven swearing by the Lord who lives forever. The same activity of the strong angel of Revelation 10:5-6 also raised "his right hand to heaven and swore by Him, who lives forever." So I believe that the strong angel is Michael.

The angel holds a small scroll in hand and declares there shall no longer be a delay. The scroll, when eaten, is sweet to the taste, but bitter in the stomach.

> And I went to the angel, telling him to give me the little book. And he said to me, "Take it, and eat it; and it will make your stomach bitter, but in your mouth it will be sweet as honey." And I took the little book out of the angel's hand and ate it, and it was in my mouth sweet as honey; and when I had eaten it, my stomach was made

bitter. And they said to me, "You must prophesy again concerning many peoples and nations and tongues and kings" (Revelation 10:9-11 NASB).

This scroll is a mystery but appears to correspond to Ezekiel 2:8-10 and 3:1-3. Both passages speak of a small scroll. Ezekiel's scroll had writing on the front and back. The scroll contained lamentations, mourning, and woe concerning the house of Israel. The descriptions of these two scrolls (in Revelation 10 and Ezekiel 2) are similar and appear to be the same.

The Day of the Lord is not a twenty-four hour day.

The scroll is a future warning to Israel. From the sounding of the seventh trumpet until Jesus returns, the Jewish people experience lamentations, mourning, and woe. More of the lamentations prophesied about Israel are found in the Book of Lamentations and correspond to end time events of the Day of the Lord.

The Day of the Lord is not a twenty-four hour day, but a season of time. A time of doom and gloom when the Lord pours out His anger and wrath on those who refuse to surrender to His Lordship. We will discover more about the Day of the Lord later in Revelation. But first, John prophesies further events.

The continuation of the trumpets is interrupted in Revelation chapter 11 by the measuring of the temple of God.

> Then a measuring rod like a staff was given to me, and I was told, "Get up and measure the temple of God, and the altar, and the ones who worship there. But, do not measure the outer courtyard of the temple; leave it out, because it has been given to the Gentiles, and they will trample on the holy city for forty-two months. And I will grant my two witnesses authority to prophesy for 1,260 days, dressed in sackcloth. (These are the two olive trees and the two lampstands that stand before the Lord of the earth.) If anyone wants to harm them, fire comes out of their mouths and completely consumes their enemies. If anyone wants to harm them, they must be killed this way. These two have the power to close up the sky so that it does not rain during the time they are prophesying. They have power to turn the waters to blood and to strike the earth with every kind of plague whenever they want (Revelation 11:1-6 NET).

I will grant my two witnesses authority to prophesy....

The outside of the temple is not measured because it is given to the nations to tread under the Holy City Jerusalem for forty-two months beginning with the takeover of Jerusalem. Other people groups instead of the Jews will have dominion over Jerusalem for three and one-half years.

I [the Lord] am about to make Jerusalem a cup that brings dizziness to all the surrounding nations…when Jerusalem is besieged, moreover, on that day I will make Jerusalem a heavy burden for all the nations and all who try to carry it will be seriously injured, yet all the peoples of the earth will be assembled against it (Zechariah 12:2-3 NET).

At this time, the Revelation passage introduces two witnesses. These men never died in the past. These two witnesses may be Enoch and Elijah who did not see death because the Lord took each up from the earth. (See Genesis 5:24, Hebrews 11:5, and 2 Kings 2:11-13.) Some say Moses could be one of the witnesses, but Joshua 1:2 reports: "Moses…is dead," therefore I do not think he would fit the criteria for being one of these two witnesses. Whoever they are, they prophesy in the power of the Word of God and the Spirit of God and have the ability to devour their enemies with fire, to prevent rain from falling on the earth, to turn water into blood, and to cause plagues on the earth. Anyone who wants to hurt the two witnesses will be killed by them.

The two witnesses will wield great power and many will despise them for it. These two men prophesy for 1,260 days (three and one-half years, beginning at the breaking of the seventh seal). They witness to their Jewish countrymen in order to cause them to return to God during the tumult of the sounding of the trumpets one through six. The witnesses finish their testimony and are killed by the beast. (A thorough look at the beast will be covered in Revelation 13.)

The bodies of the two witnesses lie in the street of Jerusalem, "the great city mystically called Sodom and Egypt where their Lord was crucified" (Revelation 11:8) for three and one-half days. The peoples of the earth rejoice over the deaths, but after the three and one-half days, life returns to them, they stand up and go to heaven as their enemies watch. (See Revelation 11:10-12.)

Then they heard a loud voice from heaven saying to them: "Come up here!" So the two prophets went up to heaven in a cloud while their enemies stared at them. Just then a major earthquake took place and a tenth of the city collapsed: seven thousand people were killed in the earthquake, and the rest were terrified and gave glory to the God of heaven (Revelation 11:12-13 NET).

At that time, an earthquake occurs, causing one-tenth of the city of Jerusalem to fall, killing seven thousand people. The rest of the people of the city are terrified, but give glory to God, because their lives had been spared. With the resurrection of the two witnesses comes the closing of the sixth trumpet, also called the second woe, and a warning of the third woe (seventh trumpet) coming quickly. (See Revelation 11:13.)

THE SOUNDING OF THE SEVENTH TRUMPET (THIRD WOE)

▶ Trumpet Seven sounds and the Lord and His Christ begin to reign and the Lord's wrath comes. The time has come to reward the saints, for the mystery of God is finished. The time has also come also for the nations to be judged: an earthquake and a great hailstorm occur. (See Revelation 11;15,18.)

The time came to reward the saints, for the mystery of God is finished.

With the sounding of Trumpet Seven, we come to the midpoint of the seventieth seven of years of Daniel. (Diagram: Daniel's Seventy Sevens on page 36.) The Day of the Lord commences as loud voices in heaven proclaim,

> The kingdom of the world has become the Kingdom of our Lord and of His Christ; and He will reign forever and ever. You have taken Your great power and have begun to reign (Revelation 11:15 NASB).

The loud voices continue proclaiming God's wrath on the nations. Now the dead, those unredeemed on earth, and those who corrupt the earth will be judged and destroyed for their sinful acts. Also, it is now time for God's bondservants, the prophets, saints, and those who fear His name, to be rewarded.

7

The Day of the Lord (The Wrath of God)

The Day of the Lord is a season of time of gloom and doom when the Lord pours out His anger on those who refuse to surrender to His Lordship with the intent of repentance and turning to Him. The struggles during this time period correlate with the Old Testament term of Jacob's trouble or distress spoken of in Jeremiah, Obadiah, and Lamentations:

> Alas! For that day is great, there is none like it: And it is the time of Jacob's trouble[or distress] (Jeremiah 30:7 NASB).

> Do not gloat over your brother's day, the day of his misfortune. And do not rejoice over the sons of Judah in the day of their destruction; yes, do not boast in the day of their distress. Do not enter the gate of My people in the day of the disaster. Yes, you, do not gloat over their calamity in the day of their disaster. And do not loot their wealth in the day of their disaster; And do not stand at the fork of the road to cut down their fugitives; and do not imprison their survivors in the day of their distress (Obadiah 1:12-14 NASB).

> On the ground in the streets lie young and old, My virgins and My young men have fallen by the sword. You have slain them in the day of Your anger, You have slaughtered, not sparing. You did call as in the day of an appointed time My terrors on every side; and there was no one who escaped or survived in the day of the Lord's anger. Those whom I bore and reared, My enemy annihilated them (Lamentations 2:21-22 NASB).

You have slain them in the day of Your anger.

More of the lamentations prophesied about Israel are found in the book of Lamentations and also correspond to end time events of the Day of the Lord. As we continue through the prophesies of Revelation, more concerning the Day of the Lord will unfold.

Joel prophesied certain events must take place before the Day of the Lord. (See Joel 2:28-31.) Wondrous events will occur.

- Display of wonders in the sky and on earth with blood, fire, and smoke (experienced in the sixth seal, second trumpet, and sixth trumpet).

- The sun will turn to darkness (experienced in the Sixth Seal and Fourth Trumpet).

- The moon will turn blood red (experienced in the Sixth Seal).

Malachi predicts Elijah will come before the Day of the Lord. (See Malachi 4:4.)

A day of judgment and destruction of ungodly men.

The Old Testament is full of references concerning the time called the Day of the Lord. As we investigate further, we see with clear knowledge that the time of the Day of the Lord is not a pleasurable era. The passages are replete with descriptions of horrific, fearful, and hopeless conditions on earth at this span of time. Observe some of the descriptive language used in these references: destruction, cruel fury, desolation, punishment, trembling, shaking, violent winds, doom for the nations, food is cut off, fires, darkness, earthquakes, judgment, gloom, trouble, distress, war, terrifying..

The New Testament also mentions the Day of the Lord. Three references are found that represent this time: the Day of the Lord will come "like a thief in the night and destruction will come…suddenly" (1 Thessalonians 5:2-3); the Day of the Lord will come when "the man of lawlessness is revealed" who comes with "the activity of Satan" (2 Thessalonians 2:3-4, 8-12); and it is a "day of judgment and destruction of ungodly men" (2 Peter 3:7, 10-12).

With the emphasis of these passages, it is clear that the terror of the Day of the Lord is to be avoided because of its severity. I entreat you, dear reader, to examine your life. Are you among those who have humbled themselves before Almighty God, turned from sin to walk God's way by receiving redemption through Jesus' blood sacrifice for sin? If you have not bowed to Almighty God, I urge you to now surrender your life to Him and receive redemption by accepting God's gift of forgiveness of sin and the indwelling of God's Spirit. Call upon His name for forgiveness of sin today while you still can.

For more clarity regarding Elijah being one of the two witnesses:

Diagram: THE DAY OF THE LORD - PAGE 47

The Day of the LORD

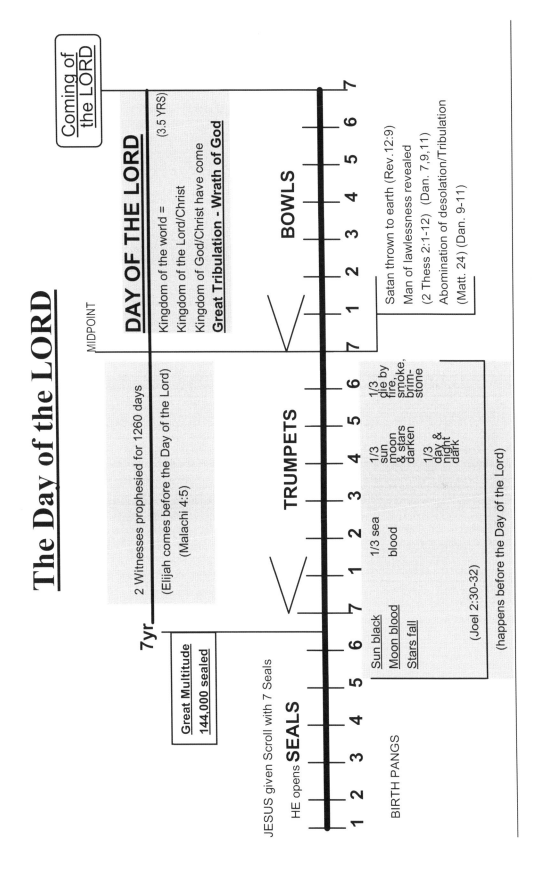

Coming of the LORD

DAY OF THE LORD

(3.5 YRS)

Kingdom of the world =
Kingdom of the Lord/Christ
Kingdom of God/Christ have come
Great Tribulation - Wrath of God

MIDPOINT

BOWLS

7 1 2 3 4 5 6 7

Satan thrown to earth (Rev.12:9)
Man of lawlessness revealed
(2 Thess 2:1-12) (Dan. 7,9,11)
Abomination of desolation/Tribulation
(Matt. 24) (Dan. 9-11)

2 Witnesses prophesied for 1260 days

(Elijah comes before the Day of the Lord)
(Malachi 4:5)

7yr

TRUMPETS

7 1 2 3 4 5 6

1/3 sea blood

1/3 sun moon & stars darken

1/3 day & night dark

1/3 die by fire, smoke, brim-stone

(Joel 2:30-32)

(happens before the Day of the Lord)

**Great Multitude
144,000 sealed**

SEALS

1 2 3 4 5 6

JESUS given Scroll with 7 Seals

HE opens **SEALS**

BIRTH PANGS

Sun black
Moon blood
Stars fall

THE WOMAN
(RIGHTEOUS ISRAEL)

Revelation 12 introduces a woman with a brief summary of her existence in verses 1-2 and 4-6.

> A great sign appeared in heaven: a woman clothed with the sun, with the moon under her feet and a crown of twelve stars on her head. She was pregnant and cried out in pain as she was about to give birth (Revelation 12:1-2 NIV).

> Its tail swept a third of the stars out of the sky and flung them to the earth. The dragon stood in front of the woman who was about to give birth, so that it might devour her child the moment he was born. She gave birth to a son, a male child, who "will rule all the nations with an iron scepter." And her child was snatched up to God and to his throne. The woman fled into the wilderness to a place prepared for her by God, where she might be taken care of for 1,260 days (Revelation 12:4-6 NIV).

She gave birth to a son who "will rule all the nations..."

The woman described as "clothed with the sun, and the moon under her feet, and on her head a crown of twelve stars" is a depiction of the nation of Israel, which corresponds to the dream that Joseph recorded in Genesis 37:9-10. The dream revealed Jacob, or Israel, as the sun, Joseph's mother as the moon, and the male offspring as the stars. Their union produced twelve sons making up the nation of Israel.

The nation of Israel produced another male offspring—Jesus—who is to rule all nations with a "rod of iron" and "was caught up to God and His throne." The woman—righteous Israel—later flees to "a place prepared by God" to be nourished and protected for 1,260 days (three and one-half years). This illustration gives a brief history of the nation of Israel from its beginning to the end of the age when Jesus returns to rule and reign over the nations.

Another character described in this chapter is the great red dragon. This great dragon, identified as the devil, or Satan, spars with the angel Michael, but is defeated and thrown to earth with the evil angels who follow the dragon (Revelation 12:7-9). Satan then persecutes the woman (righteous Israel), who then flees to the wilderness away from the serpent, Satan, the devil, for the 1260 days. The dragon makes war with those who do not flee for God's protection.

These represent the rest of the woman's (righteous Israel) offspring "who keep the commandments of God and hold to the testimony of Jesus" (Revelation 12:13-17). The "rest" are possibly converts of the 144,000 sealed of God (identified in the sixth seal) and/or the two witnesses (identified in the sixth trumpet). These events are still in the context of the sounding of the seventh trumpet.

THE BEAST

LEONARD VALEEN

THE BEAST KINGDOMS

And the dragon stood on the sand of the seashore. Then I saw a beast coming up out of the sea, having ten horns and seven heads, and on his horns were ten diadems, and on his heads were blasphemous names. And the beast which I saw was like a leopard, and his feet were like those of a bear, and his mouth like the mouth of a lion. And the dragon gave him his power and his throne and great authority. I saw one of his heads as if it had been slain, and his fatal wound was healed. And the whole earth was amazed and followed after the beast; they worshiped the dragon because he gave his authority to the beast; and they worshiped the beast, saying, "Who is like the beast, and who is able to wage war with him?" There was given to him a mouth speaking arrogant words and blasphemies, and authority to act for forty-two months was given to him (Revelation 13:1-5 NASB).

The whole earth was amazed and followed the beast.

Next on the scene in Revelation 13, we see a beast coming out of a sea described with seven heads, blasphemous names, and ten horns. (The sea is identified as peoples of the world in Revelation 17:15.) This beast looks like a leopard, has feet like a bear, and a mouth of a lion. The dragon, Satan, gives the beast power and great authority to rule for forty-two months (three and one-half years) over both the saints of God (Jewish) and the nations (unbelieving people groups) on the earth. The nations worship the beast because of the great power given it.

The book of Daniel provides more information concerning this beast. Daniel prophesied to the nation of Israel and the Holy City Jerusalem. So, Daniel's viewpoint concerns the Jews. Chapters 2 and 7 in Daniel describe four beast kingdoms that will rule over the nation of Israel beginning in Daniel's time.

As for that statue, its head was of fine gold, its chest and arms were of silver, its belly and thighs were of bronze. Its legs were of iron: its feet were partly of iron and partly of clay (Daniel 2:32-33 NET).

Then four large beasts came up from the sea; they were different from one another. The first one was like a lion with eagles' wings. As I watched, its wings were pulled off and it was lifted up from the ground. It was made to stand on two feet like a human being, and a human mind was given to it. Then a second beast appeared, like a bear. It was raised up on one side, and there were three ribs in its mouth between its teeth. It was told, "Get up and devour much flesh!" After these things, as I was watching, another beast like a leopard appeared, with four bird-like wings on its back. This beast had four heads, and ruling authority was given to it (Daniel 7:3-6 NET).

The first three beast kingdoms were:

1) Babylon, the gold head of the statue corresponding to the lion;

2) Medo-Persia, the silver chest/arms corresponding to the bear; and

3) Greece, the bronze belly/thighs corresponding to the leopard.

Daniel describes the fourth beast kingdom as follows:

In that you were seeing feet and toes partly of wet clay and partly of iron, so this will be a divided kingdom. Some of the strength of iron will be in it, for you saw iron mixed with wet clay. In that the toes of the feet were partly of iron and partly of clay, the latter stages of this kingdom will be partly strong and partly fragile (Daniel 2:41-42 NET).

The fourth beast kingdom is unnamed.

After these things, as I was watching in the night visions a fourth beast appeared – one dreadful, terrible, and very strong. It had two large rows of iron teeth. It devoured and crushed, and anything that was left it trampled with its feet. It was different from all the beasts that came before it, and it had ten horns (Daniel 7:7 NET).

The fourth beast kingdom is unnamed, but described as having a combination of iron and clay legs and feet (Daniel 2:41-42) and as having ten horns (meaning kings) on its head. Another small horn (king) comes out of the head of this fourth unnamed beast kingdom.

I also wanted to know the meaning of the ten horns on its head, and of that other horn which came up and before which three others fell. This was the horn that had eyes and a mouth speaking arrogant things, whose appearance was more formidable than the others (Daniel 7:20 NET).

The description lists this kingdom as different from the other three (Babylon, Medo-Persia, Greece). The fourth beast kingdom is terrifying, dreadful, and extremely strong. (See Daniel 7:7.)

Diagram: PROPHETIC OVERVIEW OF DANIEL - Page 56

The three beast kingdoms of Babylon, Medo-Persia, and Greece have already occurred in history. However, the fourth unnamed beast kingdom is yet to come. This empire will be divided in strength, partially strong and partially weak. When combined, it will become extremely strong, dreadful, and terrifying. The purpose of the beast kingdom will be to overpower the whole earth, as well as the people of Israel. Its desire is to trample them down along with their beloved city Jerusalem where the Jews worship the Lord. The ruler of the unnamed empire will wage war against the Jewish people of God. The ruler will magnify and exalt himself and take away the ability to sacrifice at the temple in Jerusalem. He will wage war with the (Jewish) saints to wear down and overcome them for three and one-half years. This prince ruler will destroy the city of Jerusalem along with the sanctuary of the temple.

Notice the comparisons in Diagram: 4th Beast Kingdom of Daniel about the fourth unnamed beast.

Diagram: 4th BEAST KINGDOM OF DANIEL - Page 57

Sometimes Daniel 8 is not used as a reference for end-time scrutiny because of the opinion that the prophecies in this chapter have already been fulfilled. Yet clearly, three times in verses 17, 19, and 26 the text states the prophecies are concerning the end. Therefore, the examination of end-time prophecies in Daniel 8 is included.

> So he came near to where I was standing, and when he came I was frightened and fell on my face; but he said to me, "Son of man, understand that the vision pertains to the time of the end" (Daniel 8:17 NASB).

> And he said, "Behold, I am going to let you know what will occur at the final period of the indignation, for it pertains to the appointed time of the end" (Daniel 8:19 NASB).

> "And the vision of the evenings and mornings which has been told is true; but keep the vision secret, for it pertains to many days in the future" (Daniel 8:26 NASB).

Prophetic Overview of Daniel

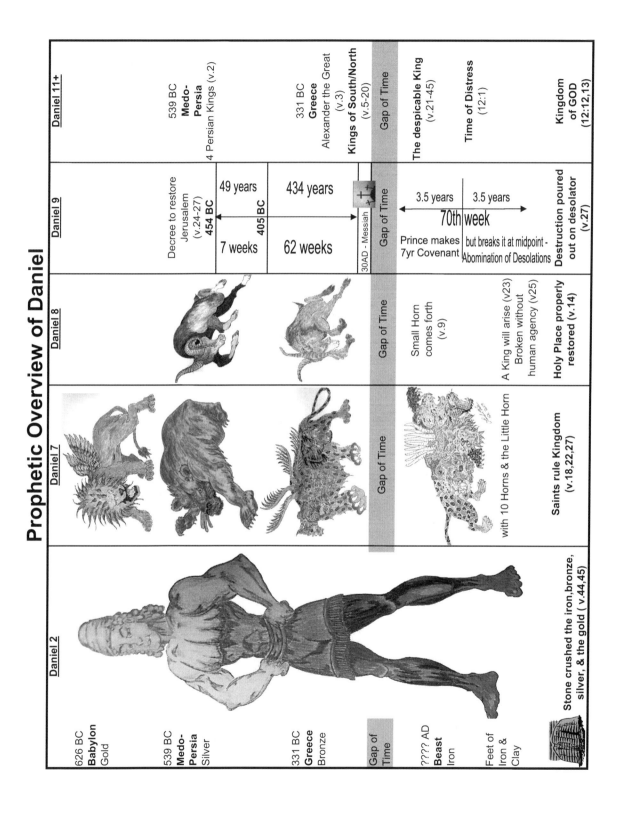

Daniel 2

626 BC **Babylon** Gold

539 BC **Medo-Persia** Silver

331 BC **Greece** Bronze

Gap of Time

???? AD **Beast** Iron

Feet of Iron & Clay

Stone crushed the iron, bronze, silver, & the gold (v.44,45)

Daniel 7

Gap of Time

with 10 Horns & the Little Horn

Saints rule Kingdom (v.18,22,27)

Daniel 8

Gap of Time

Small Horn comes forth (v.9)

A King will arise (v23) Broken without human agency (v25)

Holy Place properly restored (v.14)

Daniel 9

Decree to restore Jerusalem (v.24-27) **454 BC**

49 years
7 weeks

405 BC

434 years
62 weeks

30AD - Messiah

Gap of Time

3.5 years | 3.5 years
70th week
Prince makes 7yr Covenant | but breaks it at midpoint - Abomination of Desolations

Destruction poured out on desolator (v.27)

Daniel 11+

539 BC **Medo-Persia** (v.2) 4 Persian Kings

331 BC **Greece** Alexander the Great (v.3) **Kings of South/North** (v.5-20)

Gap of Time

The despicable King (v.21-45)

Time of Distress (12:1)

Kingdom of GOD (12:12,13)

4TH BEAST KINGDOM OF DANIEL

CHAPTER 2	CHAPTER 7	CHAPTER 8	CHAPTER 9	CHAPTER 11
-STRONG AS IRON THAT CRUSHES & SHATTERS ALL THINGS	-DREADFUL, TERRIFYING, & EXTREMELY STRONG -HAD LARGE IRON TEETH THAT DEVOURED, TRAMPLED, & CRUSHED THE REMAINING BEASTS	-SMALL HORN CAUSED SOME OF HOSTS & STARS TO FALL TO THE EARTH & TRAMPLED THEM DOWN	-THE PRINCE & HIS PEOPLE WILL DESTROY THE CITY & SANCTUARY, THERE WILL BE WAR	-KING, A DESPICABLE PERSON WILL COME IN TIME OF TRANQUILITY & SEIZE KINGDOM BY INTRIGUE -OVERFLOWING FORCES SHATTERED INCLUDING THE PRINCE OF THE COVENANT
-FEET & TOES PARTLY OF CLAY & IRON	-ANOTHER SMALL HORN CAME UP AMONG THEM & 3 WERE PLUCKED OUT UTTERING GREAT BOASTS	-SMALL HORN MAGNIFIED ITSELF TO BE EQUAL WITH COMMANDER OF THE HOST	-PRINCE WILL MAKE A FIRM COVENANT FOR 7 YEARS	-AN ALLIANCE MADE WITH HIM, HE PRACTICES DECEPTION & GAINS POWER WITH SMALL FORCE OF PEOPLE
-WILL BE A DIVIDED KINGDOM WITH TOUGHNESS OF IRON & COMMON CLAY	-BEAST WAS SLAIN & BODY DESTROYED & GIVEN TO BURNING FIRE	-SMALL HORN REMOVED REGULAR SACRIFICE & SANCTUARY THROWN DOWN	-IN THE MIDDLE OF THE 7 YEARS HE WILL PUT A STOP TO SACRIFICE & GRAIN OFFERING	-HE WILL ENTER THE RICHEST PARTS OF REALM TO PLUNDER -HE WILL ACCOMPLISH WHAT HIS FATHERS NEVER DID
-KINGDOM: SOME STRONG & PART BRITTLE	-SMALL HORN WAS WAGING WAR WITH THE SAINTS & OVERPOWERING THEM	-HOST GIVEN OVER TO SMALL HORN ON ACCOUNT OF TRANSGRESSION	-THE PRINCE WILL MAKE DESOLATE ON THE WING OF ABOMINATIONS	-HE WILL DISTRIBUTE PLUNDER, BOOTY & POSSESSIONS AMONG HIS FOLLOWERS -HE WILL DEVISE SCHEMES AGAINST STRONGHOLDS
-WILL COMBINE IN THE SEED OF MEN	-4TH KINGDOM ON EARTH WILL DEVOUR TREAD DOWN & CRUSH WHOLE EARTH	-SMALL HORN INSOLENT & SKILLED IN INTRIGUE -HIS POWER WILL BE MIGHTY		-PRINCE GOES TO WAR WITH THE SOUTH & RETURNS WITH MUCH PLUNDER -HIS HEART IS SET AGAINST THE HOLY COVENANT TO TAKE ACTION
-THEY WILL NOT ADHERE TOGETHER -IN THE DAYS OF THESE KINGS (TOES) GOD WILL SET UP A KINGDOM NEVER TO BE DESTROYED, PUTTING AN END TO ALL THESE KINGDOMS	-SMALL HORN WILL SPEAK OUT AGAINST MOST HIGH & WEAR DOWN THE SAINTS FOR 31/2 YEARS	-HE WILL DESTROY EXTRAORDINARILY, MEN & SAINTS -HE WILL CAUSE DECEIT TO SUCCEED -HE WILL MAGNIFY HIMSELF -HE WILL OPPOSE THE PRINCE OF PRINCES -HE WILL BE BROKEN WITHOUT HUMAN AGENCY		-HE SHOWS REGARD FOR THOSE WHO FORSAKE THE HOLY COVENANT -HE SETS UP ABOMINATION OF DESOLATION & DOES AWAY WITH REGULAR SACRIFICE -HE WILL PROSPER UNTIL THE INDIGNATION IS FINISHED WHICH WAS DECREED -KING DOES AS HE PLEASES, EXALTING & MAGNIFYING HIMSELF ABOVE EVERY GOD, & SPEAKS EXTRAORDINARY THINGS AGAINST GOD

In Daniel, this unnamed beast kingdom has a ruler and is called a small horn or king (Daniel 7:21); a prince (Daniel 8:24); and the abomination of desolation (Daniel 9:26). He comes to make war with Jerusalem and Israel. Let's examine these descriptions of the beast kingdom ruler.

10

THE SMALL HORN

> The horn that was broken and in whose place there arose four others stands for four kingdoms that will arise from his nation, though they will not have his strength. Toward the end of their rule, when rebellious acts are complete, a rash and deceitful king will arise. His power will be great, but it will not be by his strength alone. He will cause terrible destruction. He will be successful in what he undertakes. He will destroy powerful people and the people of the holy one (Daniel 8:22-24 NET).

In addition, the eighth chapter of Daniel indicates that the small horn king will come from one of the four kingdoms derived from the Greek empire gained by Alexander the Great, then divided after his death. From these four a rash and deceitful king will arise.

The Grecian Empire was divided among Alexander's four generals: Lysimachus, Cassander, Ptolemy, and Seleucus Nicator. My view is that the small horn king will arise out of the former northern kingdom of the Seleucids governed by Seleucus Nicator, which encompasses Turkey, Lebanon, Syria, Iraq, and Iran of today. This confirms the Daniel 2, 7, and Revelation 13:2 indicators of how the beast kingdom will look.

He will be like a leopard (Greece), a bear (Medo-Persia), and have a mouth of a lion (Babylon), all located in that northern tier above Israel. The small horn king will come from and will govern this area when he comes to power in the end time. As a ruler of the beast kingdom, he will use treachery and deceit to destroy powerful people as well as the holy ones of Israel.

Diagram: Other Beast References
(The King - Small Horn) - Page 60

OTHER BEAST REFERENCES

The King - Small Horn

Daniel 8	Daniel 11:21-34	Daniel 11:35-45
4 more horns came up in previous horn's place * out of one of them came a small horn the small horn * grew exceedingly great to the south, east, & beautiful land (Israel) * trampled down some of the host of heaven * magnified himself to be equal with the Commander of the host (Jesus) * removed the regular sacrifice (in the Temple) * sanctuary (Temple) thrown down * host given over to him on account of transgression in the latter period of their rule, a king shall arise * insolent & skilled in intrigue * will be mighty, not of his own power * will destroy to an extraordinary degree * will prosper & perform * will destroy mighty men & the holy people * will cause deceit to succeed by influence thru shrewdness * will magnify himself in heart * will destroy many at ease * will oppose the Prince * will be broken without human agency	despicable person will arise * will come with tranquility * will seize power by intrigue * overflowing forces will be flooded away & shattered * will practice deception after an alliance with the prince of the covenant * will gain power with a small force of people * will enter the richest part of the realm to distribute the plunder & possessions * will be destroyed by those who eat his choice food * will be set against the holy covenant & will take action & then return to his land At the appointed time, he * will return & will become enraged at the holy covenant & take action * will show regard for those who forsake the holy covenant * will arise & desecrate the sanctuary fortress & do away with the regular sacrifice (in Temple) * will set up the Abomination of Desolation * will turn by smooth words to godlessness those him who act wickedly toward the holy covenant Some Jews will take action	the end will come at the appointed time (last 3.5 yrs.) King will do as he pleases * exalts & magnifies self above every god * speaks monstrous thing against the God of gods * will prosper until the indignation is finished * will show no regard for the god of his fathers * will honor a god of fortresses with treasures * will take action against the strongest of fortresses * will give honor to those who acknowledge him * will cause them to rule over the many * will parcel out land At the end time * king of the South will collide with him * king of the North will storm against him * many countries will fall * the land of Egypt also * will enter Israel * will pitch his tents between the seas & the beautiful Holy Mountain The king will come to his end & no one will help

60

THE ABOMINATION OF DESOLATION

We learn more from Daniel chapter 11 because a further description of the beast kingdom ruler is mentioned, "the abomination of desolation." This ruler of the beast kingdom "will desecrate the sanctuary fortress (the Jewish temple) and do away with the regular sacrifice." This person (the ruler of the beast kingdom) takes authority over Israel, but then breaks the seven-year covenant agreement. The beast kingdom ruler will do as he pleases by exalting and magnifying himself as an exalted god in the Jewish temple—taking the place of where the Lord God formerly appeared in the Holy of Holies as the pillar of fire. (See Daniel 11:36-37.) Daniel refers to this person as a prince in Daniel 9:26. "The prince who is to come" will make a covenant with Israel for seven years at the beginning of the seventieth seven of years of Daniel 9. Then at the midpoint of this seven-year period, the "abomination of desolation," namely the beast kingdom ruler of Revelation 13, will set himself up as god in the Holy Place of the Jewish Temple in Jerusalem. (See Matthew 24:15.)

Another reference to this abomination that makes desolate is found in Matthew 24. (Luke 21 also parallels this time.)

> And Jesus answered them, "See that no one leads you astray. For many will come in my name, saying, 'I am the Christ,' and they will lead many astray. And you will hear of wars and rumors of wars. See that you are not alarmed, for this must take place, but the end is not yet. For nation will rise against nation, and kingdom against kingdom, and there will be famines and earthquakes in various places. All these are but the beginning of the birth pains" (Matthew 24:4–8 ESV).

> Therefore when you see the abomination of desolation which was spoken of through Daniel the prophet, standing in the holy place.... (Matthew 24:15a NASB).

See to it that no one leads you astray.

61

If the revelation of the "abomination of desolation" coincides with the revealing of the beast kingdom ruler of Revelation 13, let us examine what other information can be derived from Matthew 24 and Luke 21. With the birth pangs come wars and rumors of war, nations (people groups) against nations, even family members against other family members hating one another, and kingdoms against kingdoms. Not only will there be upheaval between the people of the earth, but upheaval also on the earth itself, such as great earthquakes, famines, and plagues. Luke 21:11 also mentions "terrors and great signs from heaven." The birth pangs, I believe, will be the occurrences of Seals 1-7.

Consequently, Jerusalem will be surrounded by armies. (See Luke 21:20.) As a result, Jesus instructs those in the city of Jerusalem to depart promptly, even not to retrieve any belongings. Those working in the field should not return to the city for a cloak. And those in Judea outside the city are to go to the mountains. (See Matthew 24:16-20.) Luke 21:22-24 describes these days as the "days of vengeance…with great distress and wrath to his people" so as to "fall by the sword" and "Jerusalem will be trampled underfoot by the nations" of the earth. Matthew 24:21 describes this time as "a great tribulation such as has not occurred since the beginning of the world until now nor ever shall." These descriptions would coincide with the last half of the seventieth seven of years (3 ½ yrs.) of Daniel when the beast kingdom ruler breaks the covenant agreement with Israel, and culminate with "signs in the sun, moon, and stars" (Luke 21:25) and "the powers of the heavens" being shaken (Matthew 24:29).

DIAGRAM: COMPARISON/PARALLELS OF
MATTHEW 24 AND LUKE 21 - PAGE 63

DIAGRAM: TIMING OF EVENTS IN
MATTHEW 24 - PAGE 64

Comparison/Parallels of Matthew 24 and Luke 21

Matthew 24	Luke 21
VS. 2: Jesus says, "Do you see these things? Not one stone shall be left upon another which will not be torn down."	VS. 6: Jesus says, "As for these things you are looking at, the days will come in which there will not be left one stone upon another which will not be torn down."
VS. 3: Disciples ask, "When will these things be and what will be the sign....?"	VS. 7: Disciples questioned, "when will these things be? And what will be the sign...?"
VS. 4-5: Jesus answered, "See to it that no one misleads you. For many will come in My name...." "	VS. 8: He said, " See to it that you be not mislead, for many will come in My name...."
VS. 6: And you will be hearing of wars and rumors of wars; see that you are not frightened, for those things must take place, but that is not yet the end.	VS. 9: And when you hear of wars and disturbances, do not be terrified: for these things must take place first, but the end does not follow immediately.
VS. 7: For nation will rise against nation, and kingdom against kingdom, and in various places there will be famines and earthquakes.	VS. 10-11: Nation will rise against nation, and kingdom against kingdom, and there will be great earthquakes, and in various places plagues and famines, and there will be terrors and great signs from heaven.
VS. 9-10: Then they will deliver you to tribulation, and will kill you and you will be hated by all nations on account of My name.	VS. 16-17: But you will be delivered up...and will put some of you to death and you will be hated by all on account of My name.
VS. 13: But the one who endures to the end he shall be saved.	VS. 19: By your endurance you will gain your lives.
VS. 15-18: When you see the Abomination of Desolation, which was spoken of through Daniel the prophet, standing in the holy place, then let those who are in Judea flee to the mountains: ...let him who is in the field not turn back.	VS. 20-22: When you see Jerusalem, surrounded by armies, then recognize that her desolation is at hand. Then let those who are in Judea flee to the mountains... and let not those who are in the country enter the city.
VS. 19-22: But woe to those who are with child and to those who nurse babes in those days. Then there will be a great tribulation such as has not occurred since the beginning of the world until now nor ever shall.	VS. 23-24: Woe to those who are with child and those who nurse babes in those days; for there will be great distress upon the land and wrath to this people, and they will fall by the edge of the sword.
VS. 29-30: ...the sun will be darkened, and the moon will not give its light, and the stars will fall from the sky, and the powers of the heavens will be shaken... they will see the Son of Man coming on the clouds of the sky with power and great glory.	VS. 25-27: There will be signs in sun, moon and stars, and upon the earth dismay among nations; ...for the powers of the heavens will be shaken. And then they will see the Son of Man coming in a cloud with power and great glory.
VS. 32-35: ...when you see all these things, recognize that He is near, right at the door. Truly, I say to you, this generation will not pass away until all these things take place.	VS. 28-32: But when you see these things begin to take place, straighten up and lift up your heads, because your redemption is drawing near. Truly I say to you, this generation will not pass away until all things take place.

63

Timing of Events in Matthew 24

Event	Matthew 24:4-14	Matthew 24:15-30
Birth Pangs	4 - see to it none misleads you 5 - many will come in My Name & mislead many 6 - hear of wars / rumors of wars, see that you are not frightened 7 - nation against nation, kingdom against kingdom, famines & earthquakes	
Midpoint of last 7 years		15 - Abomination of Desolation stands in Holy Place 16 - Judeans flee to the mountains
Last 3.5 years	9 - deliver you to tribulation / killed / hated by all nations 10 - many fall away / deliver up / hate one another 11 - many false prophets arise / mislead many 12 - lawlessness increases / people's love grows cold	21 - great tribulation 24 - false christs/prophets will arise, show great signs/wonders to mislead 28 - where the corpse is, the vultures gather 29 - sun/moon darkened, stars fall, powers of heavens shaken
The End / Coming of the LORD	13 - one who endures to the end will be saved 14 - gospel of the kingdom preached in whole world to all nations, then the end will come	30 - sign of the Son of Man will appear in the sky with power and much glory

THE MAN OF LAWLESSNESS

Paul mentioned the beast kingdom ruler in 2 Thessalonians.

> Let no one in any way deceive you, for it [the Day of the Lord, 2 Thessalonians 2:2] will not come unless the apostasy comes first, and the man of lawlessness is revealed, the son of destruction, who opposes and exalts himself above every so-called god or object of worship, so that he takes his seat in the temple of God, displaying himself as being God (NASB).

Paul named the beast kingdom ruler as the man of lawlessness who is also associated with the Day of the Lord. (See 2 Thessalonians 2:2.) According to this passage, this man of lawlessness will not be revealed until an apostasy comes. The word apostasy means "a departure, a falling away, a forsaking." In my opinion, this prediction does not refer to a falling away or a forsaking from faith of the Church. At the time the apostasy occurs and the Day of the Lord is initiated, the church has already been caught away to be with the Lord after the sixth seal is broken.

The Day of the Lord commences at the seventh trumpet sounding. Using this time frame, the falling away could be the Jews who form a covenant agreement in deception with the man of lawlessness, the beast kingdom ruler, who deceives them and later breaks the agreement. (See Daniel 9:27.) He then becomes the Jews' mortal enemy. The beast kingdom ruler then "takes the seat in the temple of God," saying he is God.

DIAGRAM: OTHER BEAST REFERENCES (ABOMINATION OF DESOLATION/MAN OF LAWLESSNESS/THE BEAST) - PAGE 66

OTHER BEAST REFERENCES

The Abomination of Desolation	Man of Lawlessness	THE BEAST
Matthew 24	2 Thessalonians 2	Revelation 13
Many will come in My Name saying, "I am the Christ," and mislead many	The Day of the Lord will not come unless the apostasy comes first	Beast comes up out of the sea * had 10 horns with 10 diadems & 7 heads with
Wars, famines, earthquakes are merely the beginning of birth pangs	Then the man of lawlessness is revealed * called son of destruction	* body like a leopard * feet like a bear * mouth like a lion
Then some tribulation & lawlessness * the one who endures to the end will be saved	* opposed & exalts self above every god or object of worship * takes seat in Temple of God displaying self as being God	* the dragon gave the beast power & throne & great authority * had an apparent fatal wound on one of its heads that healed
When you see the Abomination of Desolation standing in the Holy Place * let those in Judea flee	* activity in accordance with Satan * performs with powerful signs & wonders * performs with all deception of wickedness	* whole earth amazed & followed * was given a mouth speaking arrogant words & blasphemies
Then great tribulation such as has not occurred since the Creation until now * unless those days had been cut short no life would have been saved * days will be cut short for the elect		* given authority to act for 42 months * blasphemes God, His Name & His people * was permitted to make war with the saints & overcome them
Many false Christs & false prophets will arise to mislead even the elect		* was given authority over every tribe, people, tongue, & nation * all who dwell on the earth will worship him, whose names are not in the Lamb's Book of Life
Immediately after the Tribulation * the sun & moon will be darkened * the stars will fall from the sky * powers of the heavens will be shaken		
Then the Son of Man will appear * all the tribes of the earth will mourn * He will send angels to gather His elect		

THE ASSYRIAN OR THE KING OF BABYLON

There are other references which many scholars think may possibly be descriptions of the small horned king. These include Isaiah 10:24, Isaiah 14:24-25, Isaiah 31:8, Hosea 11:5-6, and Micah 5:5-6. The title which is given to the beast kingdom ruler in these passages of Scripture is the Assyrian and/or the king of Babylon. I agree that these passages should be included simply because some of these prophecies have not yet been fulfilled.

> The Assyrian will fall by a sword not of man, and a sword not of man will devour him, so he will not escape the sword, and his young men will become forced laborers (Isaiah 31:8 NASB).

The Assyrian will fall by a sword not of man.

The ancient Assyrians were seized by mere men—the men of Babylon. Therefore, this passage is referring to something other than ancient Babylon. Since the prophecy has not yet come into reality, it will be realized later with the beast kingdom ruler as the Assyrian/king of Babylon falling by the sword of the Lord.

Further support of this idea is found in Micah 5:6 which states it is the Lord who will deliver the Israelites from the Assyrian when he attacks and tramples Israel's land. Biblical history records that Israel was taken captive by the Assyrians and the Lord did not deliver Israel in that time. So, this prophecy is yet to come. I think the Lord will destroy the beast kingdom with its leader called the Assyrian/ king of Babylon and deliver Israel when He comes back to rule and reign on the earth. He will fulfill the prophecy declared. This idea affirms the northern area from Israel as the location of where the beast kingdom ruler originates.

THE BEAST KINGDOMS REVEALED

Revelation contains further information about the beast kingdom. Let's consider all the facts before moving forward. Revelation chapter 17 gives us some of these facts.

> The beast that you saw was, and is not, and is about to come up out of the abyss and go to destruction. And those who dwell on the earth, whose name has not been written in the book of life from the foundation of the world, will wonder when they see the beast, that he was and is not and will come (Revelation 17:8 NASB).

First we learn that the beast kingdom "was and is not." The beast kingdom once existed, but was smitten to death and then healed.

> I saw one of his [kingdom] heads as if it had been slain, and his fatal wound was healed. And the whole earth was amazed and followed after the beast [kingdom] (Revelation 13:3 NASB).

The beast kingdom existed in the past as Babylon, Medo-Persia, and Greece. View maps of these ancient kingdoms in diagrams on pages 70 and 71. The preexisting beast kingdoms no longer have any authority, fulfilling the phrase "as if it [the kingdom] had been slain." The second thing we learn from Revelation 17:8 is that the beast kingdom "is about to come up out of the abyss and go to destruction." After a space of time, the "fatal wound was healed" (Revelation 13:3) and "is about to come up out of the abyss" (Revelation 17:8) reviving the beast kingdom to become powerful again. When revived, the beast kingdom will receive its power from the ruler over the abyss—Satan, the devil. The beast kingdom is given authority for three and one-half years, but in the end it is destined to "go to destruction" (Revelation 17:8).

The beast will receive his power from Satan.

DIAGRAMS: MAPS OF ANCIENT KINGDOMS - PAGES 70 AND 71

Maps of Ancient Kingdoms

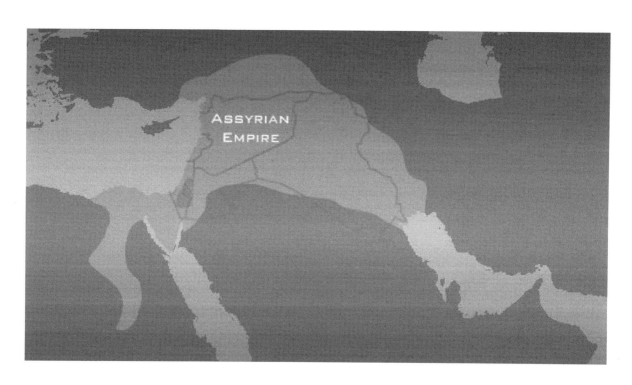

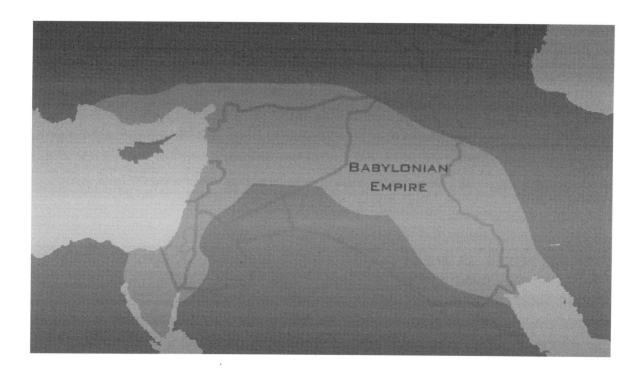

Maps of Ancient Kingdoms

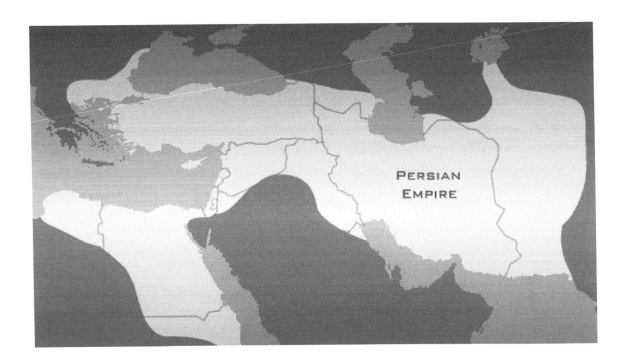

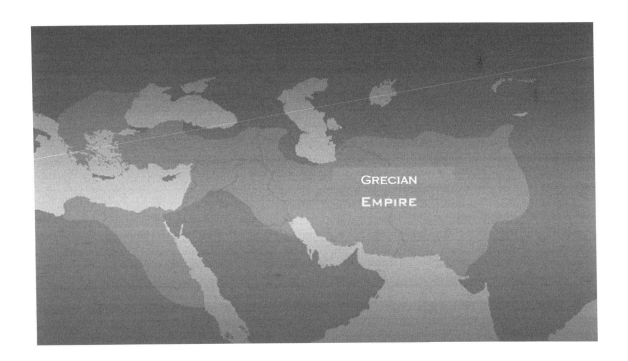

Both chapters (Revelation 13 and 17) mention the beast kingdom as heads. According to Revelation 17:9-10, these heads are kings of a kingdom.

> Here is the mind, which has wisdom. The seven heads are seven mountains, on which the woman sits, and they are seven kings; five have fallen, one is, the other has not yet come; and when he comes, he must remain a little while (Revelation 17:9-10 NASB).

Seven kings (heads of kingdoms) have ruled or will rule over Israel, five (kings/heads of kingdoms) have fallen. These five are past kingdoms that ruled over Israel: Egypt, Assyria, Babylon, Medo-Persia, and Greece. Egypt ruled over Israel from 1875 B.C. until Israel's release from captivity in 1445 B.C. Israel ruled itself for many years until the northern kingdom rebelled against God, so the Lord sent Assyria to overcome and rule them from 722 B.C. to 612 B.C. Babylon then invaded Israel and ruled from 605 B.C. to 538 B.C. With combined forces, the Medes and the Persians overtook Babylon and Israel and ruled from 538 B.C. to 331 B.C. Then the kingdom of Greece conquered the land and ruled from 331 B.C. to 63 B.C.

The beast is dreadful, terrifying, and strong, but defeated.

The sixth kingdom to rule over Israel is Rome, declared as "one is" in Revelation 17:10, which was in control as John wrote the Revelation. The seventh kingdom is the kingdom of the beast that "has not yet come" (Revelation 17:10). The beast kingdom's ruler is also known as the small horn king, the abomination of desolation, the Assyrian/king of Babylon, the man of lawlessness, and the antichrist. This ruler will overthrow many countries to envelop the kingdom. This seventh head (king of the kingdom) will overcome many peoples. From the seventh kingdom, an eighth kingdom will evolve.

The seventh beast kingdom of Revelation 13 and 17 is the same kingdom described as the fourth beast kingdom in Daniel. As you look at the diagram of the parallels of the beast kingdoms (page 73), you see the beast kingdoms of Daniel and the beast kingdoms of Revelation 13 and 17 overlap. The beast kingdoms of Daniel—Babylon, Medo-Persia, and Greece—correspond to the beast kingdoms of Revelation 13 and 17.

Diagram: Beast Kingdoms - Page 73

The beast kingdom which follows those mentioned in Daniel is unnamed but described as dreadful, terrifying, extremely strong, and different than all the beast kingdoms before it. The natural progression is to associate the unnamed kingdom with Rome since that kingdom followed Greece. However, this is inaccurate to

BEAST KINGDOMS

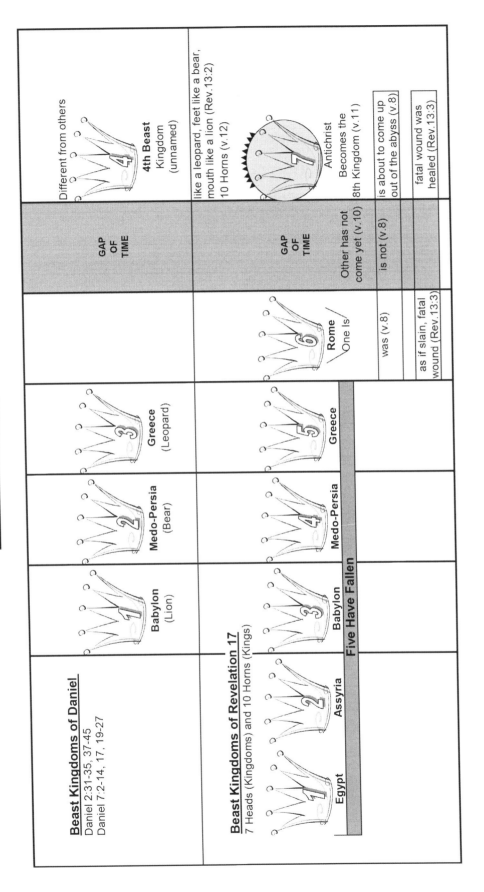

Beast Kingdoms of Daniel
Daniel 2:31-35, 37-45
Daniel 7:2-14, 17, 19-27

Babylon (Lion) 1	Medo-Persia (Bear) 2	Greece (Leopard) 3	

Beast Kingdoms of Revelation 17
7 Heads (Kingdoms) and 10 Horns (Kings)

Egypt 1	Assyria 2	Babylon 3	Medo-Persia 4	Greece 5	Rome / One Is 6
Five Have Fallen					

- Other has not come yet (v.10)
- GAP OF TIME
- 4th Beast Kingdom (unnamed) — Different from others 4
- like a leopard, feet like a bear, mouth like a lion (Rev.13:2) 10 Horns (v.12)
- Antichrist Becomes the 8th Kingdom (v.11) 7
- was (v.8)
- is not (v.8)
- is about to come up out of the abyss (v.8)
- as if slain, fatal wound (Rev.13:3)
- fatal wound was healed (Rev.13:3)

assume as the ten horned kings are only given authority to rule with the unnamed beast kingdom of Daniel. (See Daniel 2:40-41 and Daniel 7:7.)

The kingdom of Rome has never been associated with only ten kings under its rule. The unnamed beast kingdom of Daniel corresponds to the beast kingdom mentioned in Revelation 17:12 and 16. This beast kingdom rules along with ten kings during the last seven years before Jesus returns to earth to rule.

Revelation 13 and 17 also describe ten horns of the future seventh beast kingdom. These horns are kings who will receive authority with the beast kingdom for a short period of time, from three and one-half to seven years, according to Revelation 17:12.

The ten horns are ten kings.

> The ten horns which you saw are ten kings who have not yet received a kingdom, but they receive authority as kings with the beast for one hour (Revelation 17:12 NASB).

Psalm 83 lists nations which have caused an uproar against God and have made shrewd plans against Israel. These nations are a possible list of the ten kings of Revelation 17:12. They include Moab, Ammon, and Edom which are modern-day Jordan. The list also includes Edom and Ishmael which make up modern-day Saudi Arabia, and Assyria and Hagar which are modern-day Syria. Gebal and Tyre are modern-day Lebanon; Amalek and Philistia make up modern-day Gaza.

Psalm 83 Nations	Modern-Day Nations
Moab, Ammon, Edom	Jordan
Edom, Ishmael	Saudi Arabia
Assyria, Hagar	Syria
Gebal, Tyre	Lebanon
Amalek, Philistia	Gaza

This coalition of nations along with others will join forces. The ideology that unifies this coalition is the religion of Islam. These countries combine to destroy the mystery woman, the harlot Babylon spoken of in Revelation 17:5. This destruction is their unified purpose and goal. This coalition becomes the eighth kingdom.

THE FALSE PROPHET (THE OTHER BEAST)

John describes another beast in Revelation 13:11-17.

> Then I saw another beast coming up out of the earth; and he had two horns like a lamb and he spoke as a dragon. He exercises all the authority of the first beast in his presence. And he makes the earth and those who dwell in it to worship the first beast, whose fatal wound was healed. He performs great signs, so that he even makes fire come down out of heaven to the earth in the presence of men. And he deceives those who dwell on the earth because of the signs which it was given him to perform in the presence of the beast, telling those who dwell on the earth to make an image to the beast who had the wound of the sword and has come to life.
>
> And it was given to him to give breath to the image of the beast, so that the image of the beast would even speak and cause as many as do not worship the image of the beast to be killed. And he causes all, the small and the great, and the rich and the poor, and the freemen and the slaves, to be given a mark on their right hand or on their forehead, and he provides that no one will be able to buy or to sell, except the one who has the mark, either the name of the beast or the number of his name (Revelation 13:11-17 NASB).

The false prophet causes people to worship the beast.

This other beast is identified as the false prophet in Revelation 19:20, so for clarity I will refer to this beast as the false prophet. The false prophet is described as having two horns like a lamb (male sheep or ram). If the horns refer to kings here, as before (Revelation 17:16), then we have two kings in association with this lamb/ram. Perhaps this ram is in parallel to the beast of Daniel 8:3-4.

> Then I lifted my eyes and looked, and behold, a ram which had two horns was standing in front of the canal. Now the two horns were long, but one was longer than the other, with the longer one coming

The false prophet makes an image.

up last. I saw the ram butting westward, northward, and southward, and no other beasts could stand before him nor was there anyone to rescue from his power, but he did as he pleased and magnified himself (Daniel 8:3-4 NASB).

Scholars think this two-horned ram is the kingdom of Medo-Persia. (See Daniel 8:20.) If the ram of Daniel 8 and Revelation 13 are the same, then the false prophet of Revelation originates from the area of the Medo-Persian Empire.

This area would place the false prophet in close proximity to the beast kingdom located also in the northern tier—including modern-day Lebanon, Turkey, Syria, Iraq, and Iran—from Israel. Whoever the false prophet is, he gives his authority to the beast kingdom ruler and causes the people of earth to worship him.

The false prophet performs great signs, makes an image of the beast kingdom ruler, and causes people "whose names have not been written in the Lamb's Book of Life" to be given a mark on the right hand or forehead in order to buy and sell. The mark is "666." (See Revelation 13:12-18.)

THE MARK OF THE BEAST

Here is wisdom. Let him who has understanding calculate the number of the beast, for the number is that of a man; and his number is six hundred and sixty-six (Revelation 13:18 NASB).

Walid Shoebat, a former PLO terrorist and now a Christian evangelist, saw the Greek symbol that is translated as "666" in this verse. Because he is fluent in Arabic, he immediately read it as the Arabic character "bismillah" which means "In the name of Allah."

See Diagram: The Mark of the Beast to see photos of Greek symbols translated as "666"[6] and the Arabic symbol for Allah or "in the name of Allah."

The similarities are remarkable. There is at least one sect of Islam that considers "666" as a demonstration of the perfection of the Quran and proof that Mohammed is the prophet of Allah. In the "666" we find both Islam and Allah.

Diagram: The Mark of the Beast - Page 78

The Mark of the Beast

Wallid Shoebat, a former PLO and now a Christian evangelist, said that when he saw the Greek symbol that is translated as "666" in the Bible, he immediately read it as the Arabic character "bismallah" which means "in the name of Allah."

Below are photos of Greek symbols translated as "666" from FreeJesus.Net: The gold symbol (bottom and right) is the Arabic for Allah or "in the name of Allah." There is a least one sect of Islam that considers "666" to demonstrate the perfection of the Quran and prove that Mohammed is the prophet of Allah. In the "666" we find both Islam and Allah.

Hinds & Noble - 1897 - Rev. 13:18 Interlinear New Testament

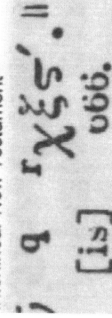

Codex Vaticanus - A.D. 350

In the western hemisphere little is known about the Islamic religion. Interestingly, this ideology has many false parallels with Christian end time views. Because of these similarities, I am including this information. See the chart below. I think you will find it enlightening.

END TIME ISLAMIC BELIEFS	CHRISTIAN ESCHATOLOGY
A savior and leader called the Mahdi will emerge with great political and military strength	The antichrist
Another religious leader, who will be identified as (a Muslim) Jesus, will arise to support the Mahdi	The false prophet
The Mahdi and the other Muslim leader (the so-called Jesus) will subdue many countries with a powerful army to dominate the world	The antichrist and the false prophet will join forces to conquer the peoples of the earth
The Muslim Jesus will kill by beheading any individual who does not submit to Islam and the Mahdi	The false prophet will annihilate anyone who does not worship and take a mark of the antichrist
The Mahdi and his leader will set up an Islamic caliphate rule and law as the only religion over those conquered	The antichrist and false prophet will change time, laws, and customs
The Mahdi will purpose to remove the Jewish people from the earth	The broken covenant agreement made with the antichrist destroying the people and taking over the land of Israel
The Mahdi will rule from Jerusalem, Israel	The antichrist will set himself up as the abomination of desolation at the Holy Place in Jerusalem
The Mahdi will ride a white horse	The seal-one rider on a white horse that goes out conquering
All Islamists are compelled to give allegiance to the Mahdi as the leader, Caliph, and Imam	The antichrist compels each to take his mark
Islamists wait for the coming Mahdi with great anticipation	All Christians who long for the return of the Lord Jesus

Islam ranks in numbers as only second to the Christian religion. However, at its present growth, Islam is growing globally and quickly becoming the largest religion. Islam denies the most basic doctrines of Christianity—the Trinity (Father, Son Jesus, and Holy Spirit), the incarnation of Jesus (God coming in the flesh), Jesus' substitutionary death on the cross, and the resurrection from death.

It also condones practicing deceit to achieve its own ascendancy. The knowledge of these facts should cause Christians to stand against this false religion in prayer to resist these ideologies of deceit. According to reports, in Iran, a DVD has been produced to inform the Muslim people of the soon arrival of their Mahdi. They are anticipating the rise of this leader. Please do not be deceived in thinking that this religion is not planning to dominate all.

SUMMARY

All these events take place in the context of the seventh trumpet sounding, the third woe, which is the mid-point of the seventieth seven of years of Daniel. This prince (the beast kingdom ruler) who is to come makes and breaks the covenant made in the middle of the seventieth seven of years concerning Israel.

The beast breaks covenant with Israel.

The events of the seventh trumpet include the Lord and His Christ beginning to reign over the world from heaven when the Day of the Lord and the wrath of God commences. A great earthquake with a hailstorm ensues. Satan is overpowered by Michael and God's angels and is thrown down to earth to give the beast kingdom ruling authority for forty-two months—three and one-half years.

The beast kingdom with its ruler and the false prophet, who originate from the area that encompasses what is now Lebanon, Syria, Iraq, and Iran, proceed to tread down the holy city Jerusalem for the three and one-half years. The beast kingdom ruler sets up himself as the supreme god in the temple at Jerusalem, turning against the Jewish nation by breaking their covenant agreement. A Jewish remnant flees to a wilderness where the God of Israel protects the Jews for the remaining three and one-half years. Together, the beast kingdom ruler and the false prophet are given authority to cause the nations of the world to take his mark and worship him.

THE MYSTERY OF GOD IS FINISHED

Then I looked, and behold, the Lamb was standing on Mount Zion, and with Him one hundred and forty-four thousand, having His name and the name of His Father written on their foreheads. And I heard a voice from heaven, like the sound of many waters and like the sound of loud thunder, and the voice which I heard was like the sound of harpists playing on their harps. And they sang a new song before the throne and before the four living creatures and the elders; and no one could learn the song except the one hundred and forty-four thousand who had been purchased from the earth. These are the ones who have not been defiled with women, for they have kept themselves chaste. These are the ones who follow the Lamb wherever He goes. These have been purchased from among men as first fruits to God and to the Lamb. And no lie was found in their mouth; they are blameless (Revelation 14:1-5 NASB).

The Lamb was standing on Mt. Zion in heaven.

In Revelation 14, at the sounding of the seventh trumpet, John describes a congregation of 144,000 Jews in the heavenly Mt. Zion singing a new song before the throne of God and following the Lamb wherever He goes. It appears these have a special closeness to Jesus in heaven much like the twelve disciples did when they accompanied Jesus in His earthly ministry. The 144,000 Jews, accepting redemption through Jesus, were purchased from the earth as first fruits of believing Jews to God and the Lamb.

These 144,000 have not been defiled with "the woman" (Revelation 14:4). Most Bibles translate the word as "women" not woman. However, the Greek word *gune* is defined as a woman or wife. Since a man is not defiled by the union with his wife (see Hebrews 13:4), I believe the translation should be "the woman." I believe this woman is Babylon, the great harlot. These 144,000 Jews have kept themselves chaste and blameless, a purity of a spiritual nature, not physical. These have not turned away from God to be united with Babylon, the great harlot. These have not taken the mark of the beast so as to worship him. The woman here will be revealed more fully in Revelation 17 and 18 as the great harlot Babylon.

The church - Jew and Gentile in one body.

The 144,000 selected Jews from each tribe of Israel performed and completed their mission to be the remaining witness on the earth of the kingdom of God. As the 144,000 first fruits of the Jews are seen in heaven with Father God and the Lamb, this event culminates as the "Mystery of God" being finished (mentioned prophetically in Revelation 10 at the sounding of the seventh trumpet). The mystery of God not only includes these 144,000 Jews, but also the church, having already been taken to heaven during the "catching away" (1 Thessalonians 4:17) also called the rapture of the church when the "fullness of the Gentiles has come in" (Romans 11:25).

Therefore, this union of both Gentiles (Ephesians 3:6) and Jews joined in one "new man," the body of Christ, (referred to in Ephesians 2:14-16) is identified as having been indwelt by the Holy Spirit of God. And so, the entire church (Jew and Gentile in one body) is in heaven with the Lord at this time establishing that the "mystery of God is finished" (Revelation 10:7). These will be protected from the wrath of God about to be poured out on the earth and its dwellers. The Church Age—the period of time from the inception of the church until the mystery of God is finished—is completed and the focus returns to the non-believing Jews to complete the last years of testing before the final return of Jesus to reign on earth. Non-believing Jews who enter God's Kingdom from this point on will have to suffer death by not taking the mark of the beast, perceiving the "abomination of desolation" recorded in Daniel as their mortal enemy, or survive the tribulation until the end of the age (Matthew 24:13) when they recognize Jesus as Messiah at His coming (Revelation 1:7 and Zechariah 12:10-12).

To see the differences between the "fullness of the Gentiles" and the "times of the Gentiles," see the diagram on page 83. These two phrases should not be used interchangeably because each is a description of a different subject.

DIAGRAM: FULLNESS OF THE GENTILES VS. TIMES OF THE GENTILES - PAGE 83

Fullness of the Gentiles vs. Times of the Gentiles

Fullness of the Gentiles	Times of the Gentiles
Romans 11:17-18 Some branches broken off/Gentile nations grafted in; Gentile nations warned not to be arrogant toward branches; root supports; became partakers with them of the rich root of the olive tree. **Romans 11:20** Jews broken off for unbelief/but Gentile nations stand by faith: don't be conceited, but fear. **Romans 11:22** God's kindness if Gentile nations continue in faith. **Romans 11:25 Mystery =** partial hardening to Israel until "the fulness of the Gentile nations has come in."	**Luke 21:20 Setting: Destruction of Jerusalem** **Luke 21:22** Days of vengeance that the things written may be fulfilled. **Luke 21:24** Jerusalem will be trampled under foot by the Gentile nations until the "times of the Gentiles" be fufulfilled. **Revelation 11:2** Court outside the Temple has been given to the nations (Gentiles) to tread underfoot the holy city for 42 months. **Daniel 9:26** the people (Gentile nations) of the prince who is to come will destroy the city and sanctuary, its end will come with a flood.
REFERS TO THE SALVATION OF THE GENTILES	**REFERS TO THE GENTILE POLITICAL AND/OR MILITARY DOMINATION OF JERUSALEM AND GOD'S PEOPLE**
THESE SUBJECTS ARE NOT THE SAME	

These events complete the sounding of the seventh trumpet. Many events have occurred up to this point in the Revelation. Some pretty horrific things have happened. Remember and consider the mortality of the times.

Well over one-half of the population of the earth will have died during these difficult times. From the opening of Seal One through the sounding of the seventh trumpet, great annihilation of mankind on planet earth will have taken place. What a staggering thought with the realization of such a horrific time of great sorrow.

❷ Seal Two

Men slay one another (a number unknown).

❹ Seal Four

The rider named Death killed one-fourth of the population of the earth with sword, famine, pestilence, and wild animals.

❺ Seal Five

Martyrs are slain (a number unknown).

▶ Trumpet Three

The bitter waters kill many men (a number unknown).

▶ Trumpet Six

One-third of mankind is killed and 7,000 people also die in an earthquake in Jerusalem along with the two slain witnesses.

SUMMARY

Up to this point in events, many things have taken place. As a review for context, let's refresh our minds with what has occurred up to this point. The birth pains began with the opening of the seven seals: peace has been removed from the earth resulting in war, famine, sickness, and death of more than one-fourth of the population with many dying of martyrdom; calamity is affecting the world including a great earthquake causing a black sun, red moon, and stars falling from the sky.

The 144,000 Jewish men have been marked for God on earth and the great multitude of the church has been caught away to heaven. Following the events of the seal openings, the sounding of the trumpets is heard: fires burn one-third of the earth; one-third of the sea creatures and ships are destroyed; people die from one-third of bitter waters tainted by the star Wormwood; the light of the sun, moon, and stars has diminished by one-third; evil forces torment mankind for five months; one-third of mankind has been killed; as well as the two witnesses and seven thousand who have fallen by an earthquake in Jerusalem. Then another earthquake and great hailstorm have occurred.

Satan gives authority to the beast kingdom ruler and the false prophet to take over Jerusalem for three and one half years. Righteous Israel flees to the wilderness to be protected by God, and the 144,000 Jewish marked men (Revelation 7:4) of God go to heaven.

DIAGRAM: THE SEVEN TRUMPETS - PAGE 86

The Revelation Of Jesus Christ

<u>THE SEVEN TRUMPETS</u>

1 HAIL AND FIRE WITH BLOOD THROWN TO EARTH, 1/3 OF EARTH AND OF TREES BURNED UP, ALL OF GRASS BURNED UP

2 SOMETHING THROWN INTO SEA, 1/3 SEA BECOMES BLOOD, 1/3 SEA CREATURES DIE, 1/3 SHIPS DESTROYED

3 GREAT STAR FALLS FROM HEAVEN BURNING, 1/3 RIVERS AND SPRINGS BECOME BITTER (WORMWOOD), MANY MEN DIE FROM BITTER WATERS

4 1/3 SUN, MOON, AND STARS BECOME DARKENED

5 LOCUSTS COME FROM ABYSS TO TORMENT MEN FOR 5 MONTHS: **1ST WOE**

6 FOUR ANGELS RELEASED FROM THE EUPHRATES RIVER TO KILL 1/3 OF MANKIND BY FIRE, SMOKE, AND BRIMSTONE; TWO WITNESSES KILLED IN JERUSALEM BY THE BEAST, 1/10 CITY FALLS, 7,000 KILLED BY EARTHQUAKE: **2ND WOE**

7 MYSTERY OF GOD IS FINISHED (CHURCH); KINGDOM OF THE WORLD BECOMES THE LORD'S AND CHRIST'S, THEY BEGIN TO REIGN; NATIONS ENRAGED, LORD'S WRATH COMES; TIME FOR DEAD TO BE JUDGED AND TO DESTROY THOSE WHO DESTROY THE EARTH; TIME TO REWARD SAINTS; EARTHQUAKE, GREAT HAILSTORM; SATAN THROWN TO EARTH ENRAGED; ISRAEL THE WOMAN GOES TO WILDERNESS TO BE PROTECTED BY GOD 1260 DAYS (3 1/2 YRS): BEAST GIVEN AUTHORITY FOR 42 MONTHS (3 1/2 YRS) WITH ANOTHER BEAST (FALSE PROPHET); NATIONS TREAD HOLY CITY (JER) FOR 42 MONTHS (3 1/2 YRS); 144,000 JEWS IN HEAVEN WITH LAMB: **3RD WOE**

PROPHETIC WARNINGS OF SIX ANGELS

In Revelation 14:6-20, we find an interlude in the action with six angels proclaiming a prophetic overview of what will be occurring next. Seven bowls will be poured out on the earth, during the last three and one-half years.

◆ Angel One flies in the sky warning the people on the earth to "fear God" for "the hour of His judgment has come," also called the Day of the Lord, the wrath of God, the great tribulation. (See Revelation 14:6-7.)

◆ Angel Two declares that Babylon the Great has fallen. (See Revelation 14:8.)

◆ Angel Three declares that anyone who takes the mark of the beast and worships him will partake of the wrath of God and be tormented forever. (See Revelation 14:9-12.)

◆ Angel Four comes from the heavenly temple and tells the Son of Man to put in His sickle and reap the harvest of the earth for it is ripe. (See Revelation 14:14-16.) This harvest is possibly the converts of the two witnesses and/or the 144,000 Jews sealed of God who die in the Lord, because they did not take the mark of the beast.

◆ Angel Five swings the sickle to earth, gathers the vine clusters, and throws them into the winepress of the wrath of God. (See Revelation 14:18-20.) This reaping includes all those left on the earth.

◆ Angel Six tells the fifth angel to put in the sickle and gather the vine clusters of the earth for they are ripe. (See Revelation 14:17.)

THE POURING OF THE BOWLS

Then I saw another great and astounding sign in heaven: seven angels who have seven final plagues (they are final because in them God's anger is completed). Then I saw something like a sea of glass mixed with fire, and those who had conquered the beast and his image and the number of his name. They were standing by the sea of glass, holding harps given to them by God. They sang the song of Moses the servant of God and the song of the Lamb (Revelation 15:1-3 NET).

In Revelation 15 seven angels with seven bowls full of the wrath of God appear. With the seven angels are those victorious over the beast, his image, and his mark. These victorious ones, who are possibly converts of the two witnesses and/or the 144,000 Jews sealed of God (Revelation14:12-13), stand and sing before the throne of God. Their victory was won by "dying in the Lord" (Revelation 14:13), giving up their lives by by refusing to take the mark of the beast (fulfillment of the Angel Four declaration when the "Son of Man reaps the harvest of the earth"(Revelation 14:15-15)). Because this group sings "the song of Moses" (Revelation 15:3), I think these individuals are mostly of Jewish decent.

In Revelation 16, a voice from the heavenly temple instructs the seven angels to pour out their bowls on the earth. The contents of the bowls contain the "wrath of God." (See Revelation 15:1, 7; 16:1.) The following sequences are in the last half (three and one-half years) of the seventieth seven of years of Daniel decreed by God for Israel and Jerusalem, the Holy City, and for all those who still dwell on the earth.

- ◆ Bowl One causes hateful and painful malignant sores upon the people who have the mark of the beast and worship his image. (See Revelation 16:2.)

◆ Bowl Two fills the sea with blood so as to annihilate everything in it. (See Revelation 16:3.)

◆ Bowl Three causes the rivers and springs to become blood. (See Revelation 16:4-7.)

◆ Bowl Four scorches the people with the fierce heat of the sun. The people then blaspheme God and do not repent of their evil deeds. (See Revelation 16:8-9.)

◆ Bowl Five darkens the beast kingdom to cause pain, for which the people blaspheme God and do not repent of their evil deeds. (See Revelation 16:10-11.)

◆ Bowl Six dries up the Euphrates River so that the kings of the east may pass to go to Har-Magedon. The dragon, beast, and false prophet release demons upon the kings of the world calling them to gather at Har-Magedon for the great Day of God. (See Revelation 16:12-16.) (The mention of the Euphrates River in Iraq is another clue of the Islamic influence.)

◆ Bowl Seven affects the air with a great earthquake as none before, and one-hundred-pound hailstones fall from the sky, yet men still blaspheme God. The great city, Jerusalem, splits into three parts as God remembers the sins of Babylon the great and pours out His fierce wrath (Revelation 16:17-21).

Notice Bowls One, Four, and Five directly affect the beast kingdom and those who worship in it.

DIAGRAM: THE SEVEN BOWLS - PAGE 91

The Revelation Of Jesus Christ

<u>The Seven Bowls</u>

 Poured out on the earth, loathsome/malignant sores on the people with the mark of the beast and who worship his image.

 Poured out on the sea, water became blood like a dead man, everything in it died.

 Poured out on the rivers/springs and they became blood.

 Poured out on the sun, it scorched men with fierce heat, men blasphemed God's name and didn't repent.

 Poured out on the beast's throne and kingdom darkened, people gnawed their tonges with pain and blashemed God and didn't repent.

 Poured out on the Euphrates River, it dried up for the kings of the east and the world, to gather for war of Har-Megedon.

 Poured out on the air, there was lightning/thunder, a great earthquake, the great city was split in three parts, Babylon the great was remembered before God, the cities of the nations fell, every island/mountain not found, 100 lb. hailstones came down and men blasphemed God.

BABYLON (THE GREAT HARLOT)

B abylon is remembered before God. (See Revelation 16:19.) Who is mystery Babylon?

Revelation 17 describes her as the great harlot who sits on many waters (peoples, multitudes, nations, tongues – Revelation 17:15) and whom the kings of the earth committed immorality with and also caused the peoples to be made drunk with the intoxication of her immorality. The immorality is the reason for Babylon being called a great harlot.

> The woman was clothed in purple and scarlet, and adorned with gold and precious stones and pearls, having in her hand a gold cup full of abominations and of the unclean things of her immorality, and on her forehead a name was written, a mystery, "BABYLON THE GREAT, THE MOTHER OF HARLOTS AND OF THE ABOMINATIONS OF THE EARTH" (Revelation 17:4-5 NASB).

Babylon the Great is drunk on the blood of the saints.

This woman, Babylon, wears purple and scarlet. She is adorned with gold, precious stones, and pearls. In her hand she has a golden cup full of abominations and the filthy things of her immoral union. Her title is a mystery, a concealed or hidden secret, detailed as Babylon the Great, "mother of harlots and of the abominations of the earth." She is drunk with the blood of the saints and the witnesses of Jesus, martyrs for the word of God and the testimony of Jesus. Revelation 17:3, 7 also indicates the woman is sitting on and being carried by the beast kingdom.

Many scholars believe that Babylon the Great Harlot is the rebuilt ancient city of Babylon in Iraq. In my opinion, this is too simplistic and does not constitute a mystery, a concealed or hidden secret.

Revelation 17:16 states that the beast kingdom and his ten horns or kings will hate the harlot so much as to make her desolate, naked, to eat her flesh, and burn her up with fire. Why would the beast and the ten kings hate one of their own cities?

I purport that Babylon is not rebuilt ancient Babylon, but a city that has characteristics of ancient Babylon. Remember that the beast kingdom ruler is joined in covenant union with Israel for seven years showing the "woman sitting on the scarlet beast" (Revelation 17:3) and how "the beast (kingdom) carries her (Israel)" (Revelation 17:7). Israel and the beast kingdom are in close association at this time. Then, in the middle of the covenant agreement, the beast kingdom ruler breaks it in deception because of his bitter hatred toward Israel.

Because Israel becomes a covenant partner with the beast kingdom and its ten kings (the kings of the earth who committed immorality with her - Revelation 17:2), they will be joined to an ungodly alliance causing idolatry or harlotry. This union is the reason for the description as a great harlot. This great city, named Babylon the Great Harlot, is Jerusalem.

Since we are using the Word of God to verify validity of thought, we will review other Scripture verses that show the identity of Babylon, the great harlot.

- In Revelation 16:19, Babylon was remembered before God to give her His great wrath. This was prophesied by Isaiah 51:17-20 and Ezekiel 43:7-8. God declared He would give Jerusalem and Israel His wrath.

- Many verses indicate Jerusalem and Israel as a great harlot, including Hosea 4:10-12; Isaiah 1:21; Jeremiah 2:20, 3:1, 6:13:27; and Ezekiel 43:8-9.

- Revelation 17:4 describes how Babylon is adorned. Similar adornments in Jeremiah 4:30 and Ezekiel 16:10-13 describe Israel as being dressed in scarlet with ornaments of gold and silver.

- Revelation 17:6 says Babylon is drunk with the blood of the saints. Verification of this is recorded in Lamentation 4:12-13 and Matthew 23:35-36 with the shedding of the blood of the prophets and the righteous.

- In Revelation 17:16, the beast kingdom hates the harlot Babylon and desires to make her desolate, to be exposed, and to be burnt with fire. Prophecies of this happening to Israel and Jerusalem can be found in Ezekiel 16:37-41, 23:22-30; Isaiah 1:7; and Amos 2:5 declaring that Israel and Jerusalem will be exposed with nakedness, be burnt with fire, be hated, and be made desolate.

- Revelation 18:5 conveys that God has remembered Babylon's iniquities. Ezekiel 21:24-25 and Hosea 4:9 remind Israel of its remembered sins and that it will experience payment for its deeds.

- Revelation 18:6 records the payment of Babylon's sins will be double—twice as much. Prophecies of this payment for Israel's iniquity are located in Isaiah 40:2, Hosea 10:10 and 12:2, and Jeremiah 26:18 as double punishment. Babylon's punishment comes as plagues of pestilence, mourning, famine, and burning fire.

- Jeremiah 19:3-9 and Ezekiel 7:3, 15 tell of Jerusalem and Israel receiving the plagues of calamity, desolation, disasters, sword, and famine.

- Revelation 18:23 says Babylon will not hear the voice of the bridegroom or bride any longer. This too is prophesied in Jeremiah 7:34 and 25:10.

- Revelation 18:24 declares the blood of the prophets, saints, and all the slain was found in Babylon. Ezekiel 22:2-13 and 36:18; Matthew 23:35, and Luke 11:47-51 all agree that Israel and Jerusalem are the source of the shed blood on the land.

- The great city is identified as the city where the Lord was crucified. (Revelation 11:8).

Revelation 17 illustrates "Babylon, the great city" as a spiritually idolatrous place, full of wicked acts. In Revelation 18, she is described from an economic viewpoint. The kings and merchants of the earth have become rich from her wickedness. The people of the great city are warned not to participate in the evil deeds done within her, because she will receive double payment for her sins, but, in pride and greediness, they do not heed the warning. So plagues are pronounced to come upon the city, including sickness, famine, and mourning. She is to experience burning with fire because "the Lord God who judges her is strong" (Revelation 18:8). From a distance the merchants and the kings of the earth cry a lament of fear and mourn over the city when they see her burning with smoke.

There are other scriptural indicators to indicate this city is Jerusalem. The next three diagrams show corresponding scriptures to indicate the parallels to Jerusalem as the great city, the great harlot.

Diagrams: Babylon (THE GREAT CITY IS THE HARLOT) - PAGES 96-98

BABYLON

The Great City is the Harlot — From Revelation	Unrighteous Israel/Jerusalem = The Harlot — From Old & New Testament Biblical Prophecies
16:19 ...to give Babylon the cup of the wine of His fierce wrath	Is. 51:17-20 - O Jerusalem! You have drunk from the LORD's hand the cup of His Anger... Full of the wrath of the LORD. Ez. 43:7-8 - ...the house of Israel ... I have consumed them in My Anger
17:1 ... the judgment of the great harlot	Hos. 4:10-12 - ... they (Israel) will play the harlot... Is. 1:21 - How the faithful city (Jerusalem) has become a harlot!
17:4 ... clothed in purple, scarlet, & adorned in gold, precious stones ...	Jer. 4:30 - .... You (Jer.) dress in scarlet & decorate yourself with ornaments of gold... your lovers despise you & seek your life.... Ez.16:10-13 - I (LORD) clothed you (Israel)... I adorned you with ornaments... Thus you were adorned with gold & silver...
17:5 ...Mother of harlots & of the abominations of the earth.	Jer. 2:20 - .... you have lain as a harlot... Jer. 3:1 - ... you (Jerusalem) are a harlot... Jer. 3:6 - ....faithless Israel... she was a harlot... Jer. 13:27 - ... the lewdness of your prostitution... I have seen your abominations... Woe to you O Jerusalem! Ezek. 43:8-9 - ... they have defiled My holy name by their abominations... let them put away their harlotry...
17:6 ... drunk with the blood of the saints	Lam. 4:12-13 - .... Jerusalem... who have shed the blood of the righteous in her midst. Matt. 23:35 - .... upon Israel may fall the guilt of all the righteous blood shed on the earth... (Also in Lk. 11:50)
17:16 ... will hate the harlot & will make her desolate, naked, & will eat her flesh & burn her up with fire	Ezek. 16:37-41 - I (LORD) shall gather all your lovers against you (Israel)... & expose your nakedness... They will burn your houses with fire... Then I will stop you from playing the harlot... Ezek. 23:22-30 - .... I (LORD) will stir up your lovers against you (Jerusalem)... be consumed with fire...strip you of your clothes... deal you hatred... Is. 1:7 - Your land (Israel) is desolate... Cities burned with fire... desolation, overthrown... Amos 2:5 - I (LORD) will send fire upon Judah & it will consume the citadels of Jerusalem.
17:17 ... to execute His purpose	Dan. 9:24 - .... been decreed for your people & for your holy City (Jerusalem)...

BABYLON (Continued)

The Great City is the Harlot	Unrighteous Israel/Jerusalem = The Harlot
From Revelation	From Old & New Testament Biblical Prophecies
17:18 The woman whom you saw is the **Great City ...**	Jer. 22:8-9 - Many nations will pass by this city (Jerusalem) & say "Why has the LORD done thus to this great city?"... because they forsook the covenant of the LORD their GOD & served other gods.... Rev. 11:8 - ... the Great City, mystically called Sodom & Egypt, where their Lord was crucified. Gal. 4:24-25 - ... corresponds to the present Jerusalem, for she is in slavery with her children.
18:4 Come out of her (Babylon) My People...	Is. 48:20 - Go forth from Babylon... Is. 52:11-12 - Depart, go out from there (Babylon)... go out of the midst of her, purify yourselves... Zec. 2:7 - Ho, Zion! Escape, you who are living with the daughter of Babylon!
18:5 ... GOD has remembered her iniquities	Ezek. 21:24 - ... you (Israel) have made your iniquity to be remembered... because you have come to remembrance... Hos. 4:9 - ... I (LORD) will punish them (Israel) for their ways & repay them for their deeds.
18:6 Pay her back even as she has paid & give back to her double according to her deeds; ... mix twice as much for her	Is. 40:2 - ... her iniquity has been removed, that she has received of the LORD's hand double for all her sins. Hos. 10:10 - ... they are bound for their double guilt. Hos. 12:2 - The LORD has a dispute with Judah, will punish Israel... & will repay him according to his deeds. Jer. 16:18 - ... I (LORD) will first doubly repay their (Israel) iniquity & sin...
18:7 ... she glorified herself & lived sensuously ... I am not a widow & will never see mourning	Is. 47:7-8 - "I shall be a queen forever... I shall not sit as a widow nor shall I know loss... Is. 54:6 - ... the reproach of your widowhood you will not remember... Jer. 3:8 - ... for all the adulteries (harlotries) of faithless Israel, I (LORD) had sent her away (divorced)... Jer. 5:12 - ... they have... said... misfortunes will not come on us & we will not see sword or famine. Lam. 1:1 - How lonely sits the city (Jerusalem)... She has become a widow... Ezek. 16:32 - You (Jerusalem) adulterous wife... Mic. 3:11-12 - ... Calamity will not come on us... Jerusalem will become a heap...

BABYLON (Continued)

The Great City is the Harlot From Revelation	Unrighteous Israel/Jerusalem = The Harlot From Old & New Testament Biblical Prophecies
18:8 ... her plagues will come, pestilence, mourning, & famine, & she will be burned up with fire ...	Jer. 19:3-9 - ... calamity against (Jerusalem)... I will make this city a desolation... because of its disasters (plagues) Ezek. 7:3-15 - Now the end is upon you (Israel)... will die by the sword; famine & the plague will consume those in the city... all of them mourning
18:11 ... merchants of the earth weep...	Is. 2:6-7 - ... filled with the influences from the east... & they strike bargains with the children of foreigners...
18:23 ... the voice of the bridegroom & bride will not be heard in you any longer...	Jer. 7:34 - I (LORD) will make to cease from... Jerusalem, the voice of joy & gladness , the voice of the bridegroom & bride... Jer. 25:10 - I (LORD) will take from them (Israel) the voice of joy & gladness, the voice of the bridegroom & bride... & the light of the lamp.
18:24 ... in her was found the blood of the prophets & saints & all who have been slain on the earth.	Ezek. 22:3-13 - You (Israel) have become guilty by the blood which you have shed... in you, they have taken bribes to shed blood... I smite... at the bloodshed which is among you. Ezek. 36:18 - I (LORD) poured My wrath on them (Israel) for the blood which they had shed on the land... Matt. 23:35 - ... upon you (Israel) may fall the guilt of all the righteous blood shed on earth... whom you murdered. Lk. 11:47-51 - ... your fathers that killed them...I will send to them prophets & apostles & some of them they will kill... in order that the Jews will be held accoutable for the blood of all the prophets...

Of all the parallels listed in Scripture and shown in the three diagrams, the most compelling reason for concluding that Jerusalem is Babylon the harlot is the phrase "in her was found the blood of the prophets and saints and all who have been slain on the earth" (Revelation 17:6 and 18:24). The Lord Jesus Christ was slain in Jerusalem. Also, in Matthew 23:35, Jesus states that "upon you (Jews) may fall the guilt of all the righteous blood shed on earth." Since Jesus is the Kinsman Redeemer who paid the price with His own blood to become the blood avenger of the "righteous blood shed on the earth," He will judge those unrighteous in Israel/Jerusalem for those slayings.

That judgment is referred to as "Jacob's Trouble" (Jeremiah 30:4-7) or the "Great Tribulation" (Matthew 24:21) thus "Babylon is remembered before God" (Revelation 16:19), with the judgment of the great harlot poured out as the anger or the wrath of God.

> His judgments are true and righteous, for He has judged the great harlot who was corrupting the earth with her immorality and He has avenged the blood of His bondservants on her (Revelation 19:2 NASB).

The righteous Jews (144,000 Jews of Revelation 14) are spared from the judgment of the unrighteous Jews because they had kept themselves spiritually pure by not entering into spiritual immorality of idolatry with Babylon the great harlot. These righteous ones received the reward with the distinction of being called "the first fruits" of the Jewish nation who were removed from the earth so that they were not among the unrighteous to receive judgment. First fruits are the initial reaping of the ripe fruit of a crop with the hope of a blessed fruitful harvest to come. Hence, a fruitful harvest of souls from the Jews is to come through tribulation, "refining and purging to make them pure" (Daniel 11:35). The remaining Jews who survive the great testing in tribulation will be counted the blessed harvest of the 144,000 Jewish male believers.

Treading the Winepress of the Wrath of God

With Jesus' avenging "the blood of His bondservants," the Bride of Christ has made herself ready for the marriage of the Lamb.

> And from the throne came a voice saying, "Praise our God, all you his servants, you who fear him, small and great." Then I heard what seemed to be the voice of a great multitude, like the roar of many waters and like the sound of mighty peals of thunder, crying out, "Hallelujah! For the Lord our God the Almighty reigns. Let us rejoice and exult and give him the glory, for the marriage of the Lamb has come, and his Bride has made herself ready; it was granted her to clothe herself with fine linen, bright and pure"— for the fine linen is the righteous deeds of the saints. And the angel said to me, "Write this: Blessed are those who are invited to the marriage supper of the Lamb." And he said to me, "These are the true words of God" (Revelation 19:5-9 NASB).

This event initiates the coming of the Lord Jesus Christ, with His bride and angels, back to earth to judge the nations who have come up against Israel at Har-Magedon.

> From his mouth comes a sharp sword with which to strike down the nations and he will rule them with a rod of iron. He will tread the winepress of the fury of the wrath of God the Almighty (Revelation 19:15 NASB).

In Revelation 19:15, Jesus smites the nations who come to destroy Israel. The nations consist of the beast kingdom countries with the ten kings and the kings of the east who join them. He rules the nations left on the earth with a rod of iron, a strong scepter of authority. He treads the winepress of the fierce wrath of God foretold and described in Revelation 14:20.

The winepress was trodden outside the city (Jerusalem), and blood came out from the winepress, up to the horses' bridles, for a distance of two hundred miles (Revelation 14:20 NASB).

An angel summons birds to "come assemble for the great supper of God" in order to eat "the flesh… of all men" in the aftermath of the great destruction (Revelation 19:17). The Faithful and True, the King of Kings and Lord of Lords, the Word of God kills the enemies and all the birds were filled with their flesh. Let us examine that phrase, "treading the winepress of the fierce wrath of God," to discover what else the Word of God has to reveal about who is involved and the outcome of the events.

THE GREAT SUPPER OF GOD

Ezckiel 38 and 39 prophesied of this time. These passages inform us that Iran, Ethiopia, Sudan, Libya, Algeria, Turkey, and others will come against Israel to participate in the Har-Magedon war. At the Lord's coming, all men "will shake at His presence," as He brings judgment on them.

> The fish of the sea, the birds of the sky, the wild beasts, all the things that creep on the ground, and all people who live on the face of the earth will shake at my presence. The mountains will topple the cliffs will fall and every wall will fall to the ground (Ezekiel 38:20 NET).

The nations who dare to come against Israel will "fall on the mountains of Israel" and the Lord will give their corpses as food for the birds and beasts of the field.

> You will fall dead on the mountains of Israel, you and all your troops and the people who are with you. I give you as food to every kind of bird and every wild beast. You will fall dead in the open field, for I have spoken, declares the Sovereign Lord (Ezekiel 39:4-5 NET).

> As for you, son of man, this is what the Sovereign Lord says, "Tell every kind of bird and every wild beast: Assemble and come! Gather from all around to My sacrifice which I am going to offer for you, a great sacrifice on the mountains of Israel! You may eat flesh and drink blood; you will eat the flesh of warriors and drink the blood of the princes of the earth—the rams, lambs, goats, and bulls of all of them, fattened animals of Bashan. You will eat fat until you are full, and drink blood until you are drunk, at My sacrifice which I have prepared for you. You will fill up at My table with warriors and all the soldiers," declares the Sovereign LORD (Ezekiel 39:17-20 NET).

This event alludes to the "great supper of God."

And I saw an angel standing in the sun; and he cried out with a loud voice saying to all the birds which fly in mid-heaven, "Come, assemble for the great supper of God, in order that you may eat the flesh of kings, commanders, mighty men, horses and those who sit on them, and all men, both free and slave, small and great. And the rest were killed with the sword which came from the mouth of him who sat upon the horse, and all the birds were filled with their flesh (Revelation 19:17-18, 21 NASB).

Since Ezekiel 38 and 39 prophesied in conjunction with the "great supper of God," the clues given in these passages confirm the time period will coincide with the battle at Har-Magedon and the judgment with the wrath of God.

In my zeal, in the fire of my fury, I declare that on that day there will be a great earthquake in the land of Israel. The fish of the sea, the birds of the sky, the wild beasts, all the things that creep on the ground, and all people who live on the face of the earth will shake at my presence. The mountains will topple, the cliffs will fall, and every wall will fall to the ground. I will call for a sword to attack Gog on all my mountains, declares the sovereign Lord; every man's sword will be against his brother. I will judge him with plague and bloodshed. I will rain down on him, his troops and the many peoples who are with him a torrential downpour, hailstones, fire, and brimstone (Ezekiel 38:19-22 NET).

The events at that time include a severe earthquake, the mountains falling, and hailstorms, which line up with the pouring out of the seventh bowl. Some consider the Ezekiel 38 and 39 prophecies to occur before the last seven years, but I disagree because of the previous reasoning listed concerning "the great supper of God."

From the comparisons of these scriptures, the treading of the winepress of the fierce wrath of God is twofold. First, God judges unrighteous Israel and Jerusalem because of their rejection of the Messiah their Redeemer, the shedding of the righteous prophets' blood, and because of their idolatry and harlotry by bringing the surrounding nations into war with them. Second, God judges and smites the nations who came up to war against Israel. (See Revelation 11:2, Joel 3:12-14, and Isaiah 34:2-3.)

For God has put it into their hearts to carry out his purpose by being of one mind and handing over their royal power to the beast, until the words of God are fulfilled (Revelation 17:17 ESV).

When the words of God are fulfilled, then God Himself and the Lord Jesus will judge the nations that come against Israel and Jerusalem.

The prophesies of Isaiah 34:6-8, Isaiah 63:1-6, and Habakkuk 3:3-7 indicate there is special judgment meted out for the land of Edom—the area located in southwestern Jordan and northwestern Saudi Arabia today. The area of Edom will be "soaked with blood" (Isaiah 34:7) and the people will be trodden down to "pour out their lifeblood" (Isaiah 63:6).

DIAGRAM: PARALLELS OF TREADING THE WINEPRESS OF THE FIERCE WRATH OF GOD - PAGE 106

With the coming of the Lord Jesus in the clouds back to the earth, where "every eye will see Him, even those (the Jewish nation) who pierced Him," then "all the tribes (left alive) of the earth will mourn over Him" (Revelation 1:7) because they had not recognized nor accepted Him as Savior and Lord, and Jesus begins to reign on the earth.

Parallels of Treading the Winepress of the Fierce Wrath of God

From Revelation	From other Biblical Prophecies
Revelation 11:2 – " ... has been given to the nations; and they will tread underfoot the holy city (Jerusalem) for 42 months."	**Jeremiah 25:15-16, 18**– "The Lord says, 'Take this cup of the wine of wrath... and cause all the nations...to drink it. And they shall drink and stagger and go mad because of the sword that I will send...' to Jerusalem...to make them a ruin, a horror, a hissing, and a curse..." **Jeremiah 25:29** – "I am beginning to work calamity in this city which is called by My name." **Jeremiah 25:30** – "The Lord will roar from on high... against His fold. He will shout like those who tread the grapes..."
Revelation 14:18b-20 – "Put in your sickle and gather ... the vine of the earth because her grapes are ripe. And the angel... threw them into the great winepress of the wrath of God. And the winepress was trodden outside the city...for 200 miles."	**Joel 3:12-14** – "Let the nations... come up... I will sit to judge all the surrounding nations. Put in the sickle for the harvest is ripe. Come tread for the winepress is full..." **Isaiah 34:2-3** – "For the Lord's indignation is against all the nations and His wrath against all their armies... He has given them over to slaughter... and the mountains will be drenched with their blood."
Revelation 19:13 – "He was clothed with a robe dipped in blood and His name is the Word of God."	**Isaiah 34:6-8** – "The sword of the Lord is filled with blood... For the Lord has a sacrifice in Bozrah and a great slaughter in the land of Edom. Thus, their land will be soaked with blood. For the Lord has a day of vengeance..." **Isaiah 63:1-6** – "Who is this who comes from Edom, with His garments of glowing colors from Bozrah...? ... Why is your apparel red and your garments like the One who treads in the winepress? I have trodden the wine trough alone... in My anger and trampled them in My wrath; their lifeblood is sprinkled on My garments and I stained all My raiment... I trod down the peoples in My anger and made them drunk in My wrath, and I poured out their lifeblood on the earth." **Habakkuk 3:3-7** – "God comes from Teman and the Holy One from Mt. Paran (Edom). His splendor covers the heavens... His radiance is like the sunlight... Before Him goes pestilence and plague comes after Him. He stood and surveyed the earth; He looked and startled the nations."

THE THOUSAND-YEAR REIGN OF JESUS CHRIST

Satan is bound in the abyss (Hades) until the Lord Jesus' thousand-year reign is completed.

Now the beast was seized, and along with him the false prophet who had performed the signs on his behalf—signs by which he deceived those who had received the mark of the beast and those who worshiped his image. Both of them were thrown alive into the lake of fire burning with sulfur. The others were killed by the sword that extended from the mouth of the one who rode the horse, and all the birds gorged themselves with their flesh (Revelation 19:20-21 NET).

The Lord Jesus judges the beast kingdom ruler and his false prophet by throwing them alive into the lake of fire. In Revelation 19:21, the nations who have the mark of the beast kingdom and who came up against Jerusalem are then killed and go to the abyss of Hades.

Then I saw an angel descending from heaven, holding in his hand the key to the abyss and a huge chain. He seized the dragon—the ancient serpent, who is the devil and Satan—and tied him up for a thousand years. The angel then threw him into the abyss and locked and sealed it so that he could not deceive the nations until the one thousand years were finished (Revelation 20:1-3 NET).

Satan is bound in the abyss (Hades) until the Lord Jesus' thousand-year reign is completed.

I also saw the souls of those who had been beheaded because of the testimony about Jesus and because of the word of God. These had not worshiped the beast or his image and had refused to receive his mark on their forehead or hand. They came to life and reigned with Christ for a thousand years. This is the first resurrection. Blessed and holy is the one who takes part in the first resurrection.

The second death has no power over them, but they will be priests of God and of Christ and they will reign with him for a thousand years (Revelation 20:4-6 NET).

In Revelation 20:4-6, the Lord Jesus will reign with His Bride, which includes the caught away church, the two witnesses, and the 144,000 Jewish men who have already received their glorified bodies. All those who have been resurrected at this juncture include those dying in the Lord from beheading due to their refusal to take the mark of the beast kingdom and the old covenant saints who died before Jesus' death detailed in Revelation 20:4-6. At this time, the saints will rule the kingdom in the land of Israel as promised and described in Daniel 7:27.

> Then the sovereignty, power and greatness of all the kingdoms under heaven will be handed over to the holy people of the Most High. His kingdom will be an everlasting kingdom, and all rulers will worship and obey him (Daniel 7:27 NIV).

Matthew 24:31 indicates that angels bring the living Jews, called "the elect," from all areas around the world back to Israel. The tribes of Israel who survive and those resurrected will finally receive their inheritance of the land promised by the LORD to Abraham so long ago. (See Genesis 15:18.) These resurrected ones will then rule and reign with Christ and His Bride for a thousand years over the nations, the peoples who survived and remain on the earth.

> All the nations will be assembled before Him, and He will separate people one from another like a shepherd separates the sheep from the goats. He will put the sheep on His right and the goats on His left. Then the king will say to those on his right, "Come, you who are blessed by my Father, inherit the kingdom prepared for you from the foundation of the world" (Matthew 25:32-34 NET).

These people groups, survivors called sheep nations in Matthew 25:32-34, now recognize Jesus as Savior and Lord. They remain in their fleshly bodies and inherit the kingdom for helping care for God's Jewish people during their time of tribulation or distress and pledge allegiance by accepting Jesus' redemption to serve and obey the Lord (Isaiah 45:23-24; Philippians 2:9-11). But they are not among those who have been resurrected as Christ's Bride or Old Covenant saints.

> "Then He will say to those (goat nations) on His left, 'Depart from Me, you accursed, into the eternal fire that has been prepared for the devil and his angels'" (Matthew 25:41 NET).

The goat nations of Matthew 25:41 who did not help God's Jewish people in their distress nor pledge allegiance to the Lord Jesus will not inherit the kingdom of God. They are pronounced as accursed and sent to "the eternal fire" of the abyss. Jesus will be king over all the earth, ruling every tribe and every nation left alive.

This era of time, called the millennium reign of one thousand years, will be quite glorious. The earth physically will thrive in optimal conditions, much like as it flourished initially in Eden in the beginning after creation. Zechariah 14:16-18 indicates that any nations left on the earth at that time will worship King Jesus every year at Jerusalem to celebrate before the Lord during the Feast of Tabernacles.

The thousand-year reign will be a time of gladness and joy.

However, if a people group does not obey by coming to worship, their land will not receive rain. Isaiah 65:20, 22 states there will be long life in those days with "one who does not reach the age of one hundred will be thought accursed" and "as the life time of a tree, so shall be the days of my people." The animal kingdom seems to be non-violent because the wolf and the lamb will eat together and the lion will eat plants like cattle with "no evil or harm in my holy mountain." (See Isaiah 11:6, 9.)

This time will be full of "gladness and joy" and "sorrow and sighing will flee away" (Isaiah 35:10). According to Micah 4:3, "Nation will not lift up sword against nation and never again will they train for war." And in Micah 4:4, we find there will be "no one to make them afraid." Truly, this will be an experience of heaven on earth.

> Now when the thousand years are finished, Satan will be released from his prison and will go out to deceive the nations at the four corners of the earth, Gog and Magog, to bring them together for the battle. They are as numerous as the grains of sand in the sea. They went up on the broad plain of the earth and encircled the camp of the saints and the beloved city, but fire came down from heaven and devoured them completely. And the devil who deceived them was thrown into the lake of fire and sulfur, where the beast and the false prophet are too, and they will be tormented there day and night forever and ever (Revelation 20:7-10 NET).

After the 1000 year reign of Jesus, in Revelation 20:7-10, Satan is released from the abyss one last time to rally those he can deceive. The sheep nations are tested to see if they will be devoted to King Jesus. This deceived army of Satan comes against Jerusalem to destroy God's people, Jesus the King, His bride and those who live there. Of course, Satan is unable to cause any more damage because God destroys this army by fire from heaven.

The demise of Satan has come. He is thrown into the lake of fire permanently where the beast kingdom ruler and the false prophet are also.

THE WHITE THRONE JUDGMENT

Then I saw a large white throne and the One who was seated on it; the earth and the heaven fled from His presence, and no place was found for them. And I saw the dead, the great and the small, standing before the throne. Then books were opened, and another book was opened—the book of life. So the dead were judged by what was written in the books, according to their deeds (Revelation 20:11-12 NET).

Another book was opened -- the book of life.

After the glorious thousand-year reign of Christ on the earth, there will be the Great White Throne judgment described in Revelation 20:11-15. Those judged will be the wicked unredeemed dead imprisoned in Hades from the beginning of time. Each will come before God to give an account of evil deeds done and will receive just recompense according to those evil deeds and that they did not accept the redemption provided by the Lord Jesus. Their names will not be found written in the book of life. These will be thrown into the lake of fire, along with death and Hades forevermore, never to be released.

DESTINATIONS OF PERSONS AFTER DEATH

In the body of Christ Jesus, there is much interest as to the destination of everyone who dies. Because an understanding of this thought-provoking subject is desirable, let us consider where both redeemed believers in Jesus Christ and unredeemed unbelievers are located after death.

Luke 16:19-31 gives some insight into the region of departed spirits. This place is called Hades in the Greek and Sheol in the Hebrew languages. This region is located deep within the earth and is a real place. Jesus isn't speaking in a parable in this passage. Notice the mention of the reality of the senses in the text. The description lists seeing, speaking, hearing, and recognizing one another. There are sensations of feeling torment and agony as well as comfort. There is extreme thirsting in areas of this place. This is a real place.

So let us reflect on the outcome of each one after death. As a guide, refer to the five diagrams about the destinations of persons after death.

DIAGRAM: WHAT HAPPENS AFTER DEATH (1) - PAGE 114

The location of the region of departed spirits below the earth (Hades or Sheol) is divided into two areas. One side is called Abraham's Bosom and is separated from the other side by a chasm. In Abraham's Bosom, there seems to be comfort.

The other side is considered a place of agony and torment. Before Jesus' resurrection, the spirits of believing saints who looked forward to redemption in Messiah went to the Abraham's Bosom side of Hades/Sheol. Before Jesus' resurrection, the spirits of unbelievers went to the torment, agony, and fire side of Hades/Sheol.

When Jesus died on the cross, was buried, resurrected, and ascended, He paid the redemption price for sin. Since the payment of sin had been paid, Jesus retrieved the righteous spirits in Abraham's Bosom side of Hades and took them to heaven

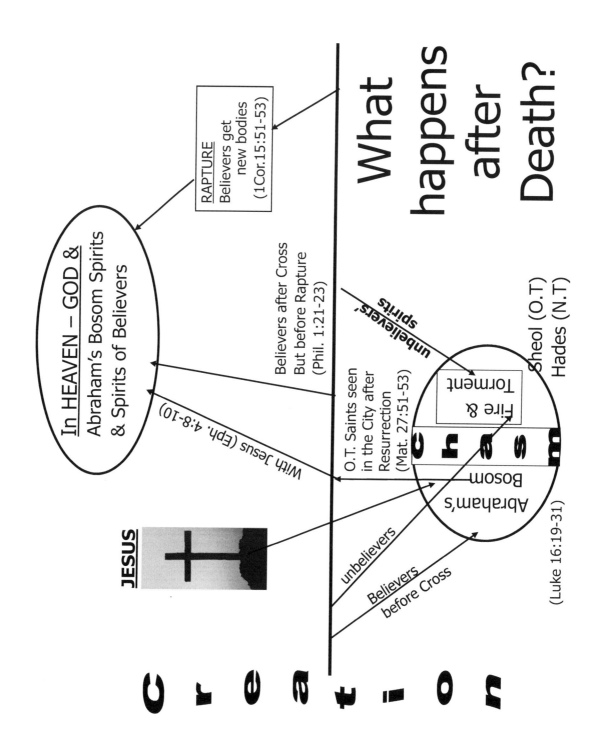

What happens after Death?

RAPTURE
Believers get
new bodies
(1Cor.15:51-53)

In HEAVEN – GOD &
Abraham's Bosom Spirits
& Spirits of Believers

Believers after Cross
But before Rapture
(Phil. 1:21-23)

With Jesus (Eph. 4:8-10)

O.T. Saints seen
in the City after
Resurrection
(Mat. 27:51-53)

unbelievers' spirits

Sheol (O.T)
Hades (N.T)

Fire & Torment

Abraham's Bosom

JESUS

unbelievers

Believers
before Cross

(Luke 16:19-31)

creation

with Him. Ephesians 4:8-10 refers to this time when Jesus ascended to heaven and explains that He led the captured spirits in Abraham's Bosom back with Him to heaven. Also, Matthew 27:51-53 states that the dead saints were seen walking in Jerusalem after Jesus' resurrection giving evidence of that realization.

After Jesus' cross and resurrection, the spirits of believers who accepted redemption in Christ Jesus ascend to heaven when the person dies. Paul said that "to be absent from the body is to be with the Lord" (2 Corinthians 5:6-8). In Philippians 1:21-23 Paul stated his desire was to depart, to die, and be with Christ who is in heaven. But the spirits of unredeemed unbelievers who die after the resurrection of Jesus descend into Hades/Sheol.

At the time of the "catching away" or rapture of the church (recorded in Revelation 7:9-17), believers join together to ascend to meet Jesus in the air and clouds. The church includes the spirits of redeemed believers, who had died after Jesus' cross and are already in heaven, and the living redeemed believers on the earth. These meet Jesus in the air and receive a new glorified body "in an instant" and return with Jesus to heaven. (See 1 Thessalonians 4:12-18 and 1 Corinthians 15:51-54.)

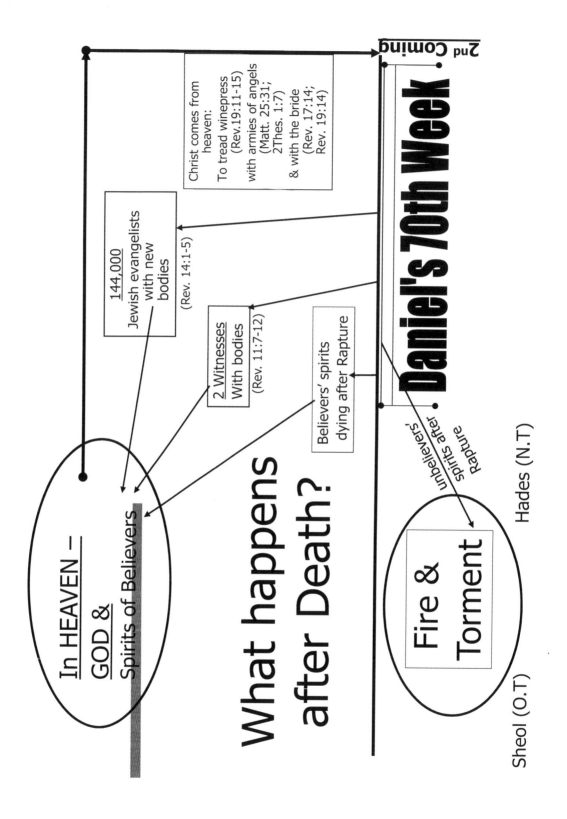

What happens after Death?

In HEAVEN –
GOD &
Spirits of Believers

144,000
Jewish evangelists
with new
bodies
(Rev. 14:1-5)

2 Witnesses
With bodies
(Rev. 11:7-12)

Believers' spirits
dying after Rapture

Christ comes from
heaven:
To tread winepress
(Rev.19:11-15)
with armies of angels
(Matt. 25:31;
2Thes. 1:7)
& with the bride
(Rev. 17:14;
Rev. 19:14)

2nd Coming

Daniel's 70th Week

unbelievers'
spirits after
Rapture

Fire &
Torment

Sheol (O.T)

Hades (N.T)

116

The next display includes the time after the taking away of the church through to the coming of the Lord Jesus back to earth to set up His kingdom. This time frame is also known as the last seven years prior to the Lord Jesus' return or Daniel's seventieth week of years.

Unbelieving ones who die during this time depart in their spirits to Hades/Sheol. The two witnesses, killed by the beast kingdom at the closing of the sixth trumpet, are resurrected when God calls them to "come up here" (Revelation 11:11-12) and are given their new glorified bodies.

The 144,000 sons of the tribes of Israel, the first fruits of the Jews purchased by the blood of Jesus, are taken to heaven at the sounding of the seventh trumpet. They receive new glorified bodies since they are considered a part of the church and described as "the mystery of God being finished" (Revelation 10:7).

When believers who accept redemption after the Rapture of the church die, their spirits go to heaven but do not receive a new body at this time. When unredeemed unbelievers die after the Rapture of the church, their spirits descend into Hades/Sheol.

Jesus Christ returns to the earth with His armies, including His Bride and angels, to remove those who have come up against Jerusalem to fight. He treads the winepress of the fierce wrath of God. The Bride of Christ, the church, including the two witnesses, and the 144,000 Jewish men come back to earth with Jesus and are already in their glorified bodies. These are the called, the chosen and the faithful.

What happens after Death?

When Christ returns from heaven, His angels gather the Jews from the 4 winds (Mat.24:31-51). It appears that they do not receive a glorified body, but are gathered to Israel, given His Spirit, & are able to reproduce (Ez. 36:22-38)

2nd Coming

Sheep enter kingdom (Matt. 25:31-46)

Goat Nations

Anyone who dies (Isa.65:18-25)

Satan bound

Beast Armies

Fire & Torment
Sheol Hades

1st Resurrection (Rev.20:4-6):
- Abraham's bosom (O.T. saints – Dan.12:1+2)
- Souls under the altar (Rev.6:9-11)
- The church/bride (Rev.7:9-17)
- Believing Jews killed after the rapture
  - These receive imperishable bodies!

1000-year reign

At the end, Satan released, deceives nations, battle of Gog & Magog (Rev. 20:7-9)

Beast & False Prophet cast into Lake of Fire (Rev.19:20)

Satan cast into Lake of Fire (Rev. 20:10)

Lake of Fire 2nd Death

Continuing on, let us consider what occurs after Jesus comes back to the earth and the outcome of those living at His return. The armies of the beast kingdom who came against Jerusalem are killed by the Word of the Lord Jesus. Their spirits descend into Hades. (See Revelation 19:21.) The beast kingdom ruler and his false prophet are thrown alive into the lake of fire. (See Revelation 19:20.) Satan is bound for one thousand years in Hades. (See Revelation 20:2.)

Then, angels gather the elect Jews from the four corners of the earth. (See Matthew 24:31 and Matthew 25:31-32.) These Jews include the righteous protected by God in the wilderness for the last three and one-half years before Jesus' return and the scattered around the globe still alive. It appears they do not receive new glorified bodies, but they are given the Holy Spirit within because they recognize Jesus as Messiah and pledge allegiance to serve and obey Him. Zechariah 12:10 describes this time as mourning, saying, "They will look on Me who they have pierced...and mourn...and weep bitterly over Him." They then inherit the land of Israel as promised to Abraham (Genesis 15:18). These continue in fleshly bodies and produce offspring. (See Ezekiel 36:22-38; 37:25-26; and Isaiah 60:21-22.)

Also, the nations or people groups left alive of the world are brought before Jesus. (See Matthew 25:31-32.) They are separated into two groups, the sheep nations and the goat nations. The sheep nations in fleshly bodies enter into God's kingdom on earth because they recognized Jesus as Savior (seeing His hands and feet pierced) and pledged allegiance to Jesus Christ. (See Isaiah 45:23-24 and Philippians 2:9-11.) They helped Israel in her time of distress, also called the great tribulation (See Matthew 25:34, 39.), and did not take the mark of the beast. Because the goat nations did not help the nation of Israel in her time of distress nor pledge allegiance to Jesus, they are judged and sentenced by Jesus and depart into Hades. (See Matthew 25:41-46.)

Next, the time referred to as the "first resurrection" occurs (Revelation 20:5). The recipients of the "first resurrection" include believing old covenant saints' spirits delivered from Abraham's Bosom when Jesus took them to heaven at His resurrection and believers' spirits who died or were killed after the Rapture of the church, but before the coming of the Lord back to earth. These are distinguished by not taking the mark of the beast kingdom (Revelation 20:4-6).

119

Both the old covenant saints and the ones who overcame the beast kingdom and its mark receive their new glorified bodies at this time. Remember, the raptured church, the two witnesses, and the 144,000 Jews have already received their new glorified bodies.

After this, the thousand-year reign of Jesus Christ on earth ensues. During Jesus' reign, the world is a wonderful place to live. The people in fleshly bodies reproduce and live long lives. Yet, if anyone dies during this time, they are considered accursed and their spirits descend into Hades. At the end of the one-thousand-year reign of Jesus, Satan is released from Hades for a time of testing of the sheep nations and their offspring to verify their allegiance to the Lord Jesus. The nations Satan deceives (again) are called "Gog and Magog." These nations deceived by Satan are killed by God by fire descending from heaven (Revelation 20:9). Satan then is judged and thrown into the lake of fire.

DIAGRAM: WHAT HAPPENS AFTER DEATH (4) - PAGE 121

Following the thousand-year reign of Jesus, it is time for the judging of the unredeemed dead. The departed spirits in Hades are gathered before the Great White Throne of God, the Almighty, for the judgment of their deeds (Revelation 20:11-15). Any one of the unredeemed dead whose name (none of them) is not found in the book of life is thrown into the lake of fire (Revelation 20:15). Along with these, Death and Hades are thrown into the lake of fire (Revelation 20:14 and 1 Corinthians 15:26, 55). These remain in the lake of fire forever, never to escape.

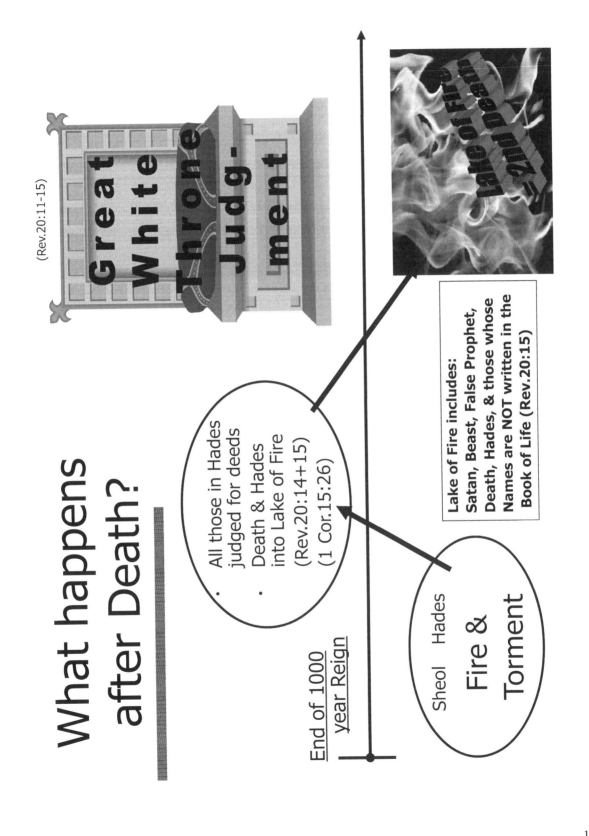

What happens after Death?

(Rev.20:11-15)

Great White Throne Judg-ment

- All those in Hades judged for deeds
- Death & Hades into Lake of Fire (Rev.20:14+15) (1 Cor.15:26)

Lake of Fire includes: Satan, Beast, False Prophet, Death, Hades, & those whose Names are NOT written in the Book of Life (Rev.20:15)

Lake of Fire = 2nd Death

End of 1000 year Reign

Sheol Hades Fire & Torment

What happens after Death?

New Heavens

New Jerusalem

The Bride

New Earth

Sheep nations & offspring are the nations (Rev. 21:24-22:5)

These are in natural bodies that eat leaves of the Tree of Life for healing (Rev. 22:2)

ETERNITY!

DIAGRAM: WHAT HAPPENS AFTER DEATH (5) - PAGE 122

After this great event, The LORD God creates a New Heaven, a New Earth. The New Jerusalem comes down from heaven to the New Earth (Revelation 21:1-2). The sheep nations and their offspring who were not deceived by Satan will live on the New Earth (Revelation 21:24-22:5).

These nations will live in natural bodies and eat from the leaves of the Tree of Life for healing to live forever (Revelation 22:2). Father God, Jesus, His Bride, and the resurrected saints will live in the New Jerusalem on the New Earth ruling over the nations, the people groups who survive the thousand-year reign of Jesus Christ.

View the sequence of all the events in Revelation.

DIAGRAM: REVELATION TIME LINE - PAGE 124

DIAGRAM: REVELATION + PROPHECY TIME LINE - PAGE 125

REVELATION TIMELINE

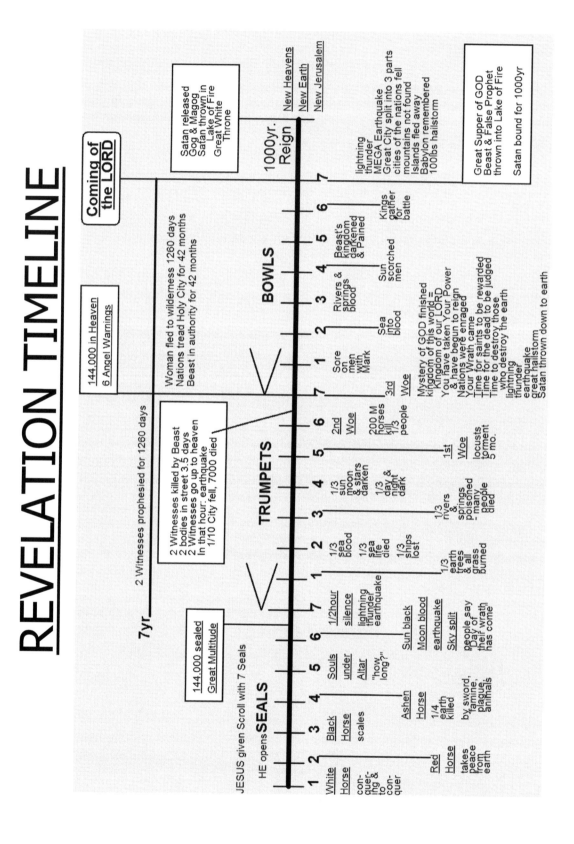

REVELATION + PROPHECY TIMELINE

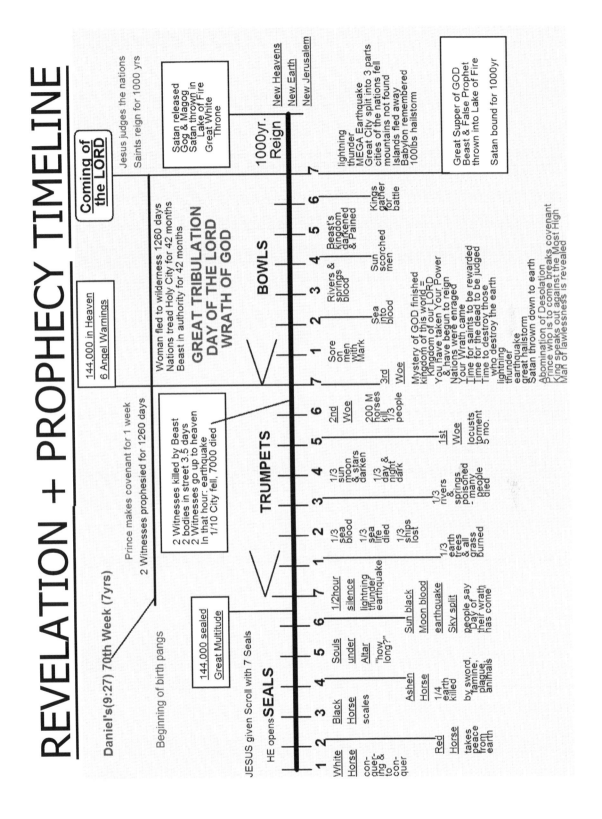

Coming of the LORD

Daniel's(9:27) 70th Week (7yrs)

144,000 in Heaven
6 Angel Warnings

Jesus judges the nations
Saints reign for 1000 yrs

Prince makes covenant for 1 week
2 Witnesses prophesied for 1260 days

Beginning of birth pangs

Woman fled to wilderness 1260 days
Nations tread Holy City for 42 months
Beast in authority for 42 months

GREAT TRIBULATION
DAY OF THE LORD
WRATH OF GOD

Satan released
Gog & Magog
Satan thrown in
Great White
Throne
Lake of Fire

1000yr.
Reign

New Heavens
New Earth
New Jerusalem

2 Witnesses killed by Beast
2 bodies in street 3.5 days
2 Witnesses go up to heaven
In that hour: earthquake
1/10 City fell, 7000 died

lightning
thunder
MEGA Earthquake
Great City split into 3 parts
cities of the nations fell
mountains not found
Islands fled away
Babylon remembered
100lbs hailstorm

Great Supper of GOD
Beast & False Prophet
thrown into Lake of Fire

Satan bound for 1000yr

144,000 sealed
Great Multitude

JESUS given Scroll with 7 Seals

HE opens **SEALS**

TRUMPETS

BOWLS

SEALS

1 White Horse
con-quer-ing & to con-quer

2 Red Horse
takes peace from earth

3 Black Horse
scales

4 Ashen Horse
1/4 earth killed
by sword, famine, plague, animals

5 Souls under Altar
"how long?"

6 Sun black
Moon blood
earthquake
Sky split
People say "Day of their wrath has come"

7 1/2hour silence
lightning thunder earthquake

TRUMPETS

1 1/3 earth trees & all grass burned

2 1/3 sea blood
1/3 sea life died
1/3 ships lost

3 1/3 rivers & springs poisoned - many people died

4 1/3 sun moon & stars darken
1/3 day & night dark

5 1st Woe
locusts torment 5 mo.

6 2nd Woe
200 M horses kill 1/3 people

7 3rd Woe
Mystery of GOD finished
kingdom of this world =
Kingdom of our LORD
You have taken Your Power
& have begun to reign
Nations were enraged
Your Wrath came
Time for saints to be rewarded
Time for the dead to be judged
Time to destroy those
who destroy the earth
lightning
thunder
earthquake
great hailstorm
Satan thrown down to earth

Abomination of Desolation
Prince who is to come breaks covenant
King speaks out against the Most High
Man of lawlessness is revealed

BOWLS

1 Sore on men With Mark

2 Sea into blood

3 Rivers & springs blood

4 Sun scorched men

5 Beast's kingdom darkened & Pained

6 Kings gather for battle

7 lightning
thunder
MEGA Earthquake
Great City split into 3 parts
cities of the nations fell
mountains not found
Islands fled away
Babylon remembered
100lbs hailstorm

NEW HEAVEN, NEW EARTH, NEW JERUSALEM

After the Great White Throne Judgment and after death has been conquered, a new heaven and a new earth are created.

I am coming quickly.

> Then I saw a new heaven and a new earth; for the first heaven and the first earth passed away, and there is no longer any sea (Revelation 21:1 NASB).

The New Jerusalem, the city of God's people, comes down from heaven to the new earth where God will dwell with them forevermore. Truly, the "first things have passed away" (Revelation 21:4). The bondservants, who overcame the world, the flesh, and the devil, and the temptation to sin and live selfishly, inherit the kingdom of God, the New Heaven and New Earth. This new city, the household of God, shines with the glory of God. Its walls are more than 72 yards thick and made of brilliant jasper in a 1500-mile cubic configuration.

The city has twelve gates made of a single pearl each and twelve foundation slabs made of different precious stones. The rest of the city is of pure gold. The throne of God and the Lamb will be in the city and the bondservants (Revelation 22:3) will serve them. They will see God's face. There will be no more death, no mourning, no crying, nor pain. All traces of the former sin-affected world have disappeared forever. God and His people will reign forever and ever.

The throne of God and the Lamb will be in the New Jerusalem.

There will be no temple in the New Jerusalem, for it will no longer be needed because Father God and the Lord Jesus will be the sanctuary. God will illuminate the city with glory so that the light of the sun and moon will no longer be needed. All the nations, the people who survived the one-thousand year reign of Jesus Christ, will walk by the city's light and there will be no more darkness. These peoples, who have sworn allegiance to the Lord Jesus (Isaiah 45:23-24, Romans 14:11-12) and had not been deceived by Satan at the end of the thousand-year reign of Jesus, will continue to live in their fleshly bodies, which will be kept healthy by eating the leaves of the Tree of Life (Genesis 2 and 3) used for the healing of the nations (Revelation 22:2).

Forever we will be dwelling with our Heavenly Father and our glorious Bridegroom, Jesus Christ, in the New Jerusalem. Father God, the Lord Jesus, the Bride of Jesus, and the resurrected saints will rule and reign for all eternity over the nations who are in their fleshly bodies. All will live in peace and harmony.

What a high calling the church and the saints have. The privilege of the experience of these promises is mind-boggling. Ponder these promises and keep them ever before you when the temptation to drift away comes. Persevere, redeemed ones, persevere. Keep full of faith and do all that is necessary to attain to all the promises of reward by the Lord Jesus and laid out in the *Revelation*. You do not want to miss this.

Revelation ends with an exhortation from Jesus. He pronounces the blessing again to any who heed the words of this prophecy. He confirms the truth of His coming, saying that it is "coming quickly, for the time is near" (Revelation 22:7, 10). With His promise of return, He exhorts and encourages, saying that He will reward everyone "according to what he has done" (Revelation 22:22). There is reward for everyone who overcomes in this life by appropriating the blood of Jesus to remove their sin. Yet, if anyone refuses the free gift of release from sin, he will not be considered a bondservant of the household of the Kingdom of God.

Thus, the one who does not repent and turn to God in faith is bound to experience the awful things described in the book of the *Revelation*. One's destiny lies in this decision: surrender to God's way of eternal life by Jesus' redeeming blood shed for the removal of sin, or refuse to surrender to God's way to receive eternal separation from God in eternal agony of death—the consequence for sin. Receive the free gift of eternal life since Jesus has already provided the way to not die in sin by loving us and releasing us from the power of sin. I beg you, surrender to God and ask Him to free you from sin and death. The blood of Jesus has paid the price for your sin. Be cleansed from sin to obey God in this life and He will bring you to receive all the good things mentioned in these pages. My hope is for you to be with all believers at Jesus' coming.

> Look! I am coming soon, and my reward is with me to pay each one according to what he has done! (Revelation 22:12 NET).

"I, Jesus, have sent my angel to testify to you about these things for the churches. I am the root and the descendant of David, the bright morning star!" And the Spirit and the bride say, "Come!" And let the one who hears say: "Come!" And let the one who is thirsty come; let the one who wants it take the water of life free of charge (Revelation 22:16-17 NET).

EVEN SO, COME, LORD JESUS.

WHO IS THIS KING OF GLORY? THE LORD STRONG AND MIGHTY, THE LORD MIGHTY IN BATTLE...THE LORD OF HOSTS, HE IS THE KING OF GLORY (PSALM 24:8,10).

ENDNOTES

1   Revelation 5:5 NASB

2   Revelation 5:12 NASB The kinsman redeemer qualifications include: 1.) must be the closest relative, 2.) the relative had to want to redeem, 3.) the relative had to have the price to pay for the redemption, 4.) the relative had to serve as the blood avenger in case of death, 5.) the relative had to have the power to restore all the land to its rightful owner, i.e. to remove all invaders, occupiers, or squatters from the land. The kinsman redeemer had the right to redeem: 1.) the land or property of the kinsman's inheritance, 2.) the widow of the kinsman by marrying to produce an heir for the deceased kin, 3.) a kinsman from slavery, 4.) and avenge the death of a murdered kinsman. An illustration of the kinsman redeemer can be found in the Book of Ruth. Jesus, as mankind's Kinsman Redeemer, fully met all these qualifications to redeem mankind from slavery to sin and death.

3   The description of the angel is perhaps the fulfillment of Ezekiel 9:3-6 where the Lord commanded someone in linen to put a mark on the foreheads of those who sigh and groan over the abominations done in Jerusalem.

4   See Revelation 7:14 NASB

5   Not only is this Great Multitude mentioned in those verses above, but also in Revelation 19:1-8. The Great Multitude is proclaiming three hallelujahs.

- Because the Lord's judgments are just and true and He has avenged the blood of His bondservants on Babylon, the great harlot, due to the blood shed of the prophets, saints, and the ones slain on the earth, which was found in her.

- Because Babylon's smoke rises forever.

- Because the Lord reigns; they rejoice for "the marriage of the Lamb has come and His Bride has made herself ready."

Thus, this is a clear and direct description of the Great Multitude being the Lamb's Bride, the church.

6   FreeJesus.net. Walid Shoebat was a former PLO terrorist but now is a Christian evangelist. When he saw the Greek symbol that is translated "666" in the Bible, he immediately read it as the Arabic character "bismillah" which means "in the name of Allah."

ABOUT THE AUTHOR

J. J. Como writes about a life-long passion of studying and researching the end times.

As a Bible teacher in a mega church in Houston, Texas, the author discovered that more in-depth information was needed to fully disciple this generation on the subject of The Revelation.

J. J. has been an accredited Bible teacher through Precepts International for more than fifteen years.

J. J. and family reside in the Houston, Texas, area.

Made in the USA
San Bernardino, CA
25 October 2013